KS1

WE BELIEVE

ISLAMIC STUDIES GUIDE 3

DR. AYMAN YACOUB
Jurisprudent & Forensic Linguist

MAHMOUD FAWZY
B.Th. Fundamentals of Religion

MOHAMMED KHATTAB
B.Ed. Languages & Education

AMMAR EL-KHATIB
MSc. Islamic Finance & Education

"AND SAY O'MY LORD INCREASE MY KNOWLEDGE"

TAHA (114)

Birmingham, United Kingdom

Azhary Press is a department of Azhary Organisation. It cultivates the Organisation's objective of distinction in research, authorship, scholarship, and education by publishing worldwide. Azhary press is a trademark of Azhary organisation Ltd.

First published in 2024

Printed in Great Britain

THE AUTHORS

Dr. Ayman Yacoub
Jurisprudent & Forensic Linguist
Al-Azhar University-Oxford University
Birmingham University

Mahmoud Fawzy, B.Th.
Fundamentals of religion School
Al-Azhar University, Egypt

Mohammed Khattab, B.Sc.Ed.
Language Department, School of Education,
Al-Azhar University, Egypt

Ammar El-Khatib, MSc.
Islamic Finance & Education
Birmingham City University, UK

Thank You

We want to express our deepest gratitude to Allah, followed by everyone involved in the publication of this book, with whom we have had the privilege of working.
Special thanks go to:

PROOFREADING & EDITING

Dr. Doaa Mohammed.
Hala Elkheyouty.
Iman Elshennawy.

AZHARY FUTURE

A heartfelt thanks go to our youngest team, who provided valuable input on the design.

Alyaa Elkhatib. Asir Yacoub.
Balquees Khattab. Basil Yacoub.
Malek Elkhatib. Maryam Khattab.
Sara Khattab. Yousof Khattab.

ILLUSTRATIONS & GRAPHIC DESIGN

Dr. Ayman Yacoub

ISBN 978-191651001-2

How to get in touch?

 info@azhary.org

 Azhary Organisation

 (+44)744-214-9581

"AND SAY O'MY LORD INCREASE MY KNOWLEDGE"

TAHA (114)

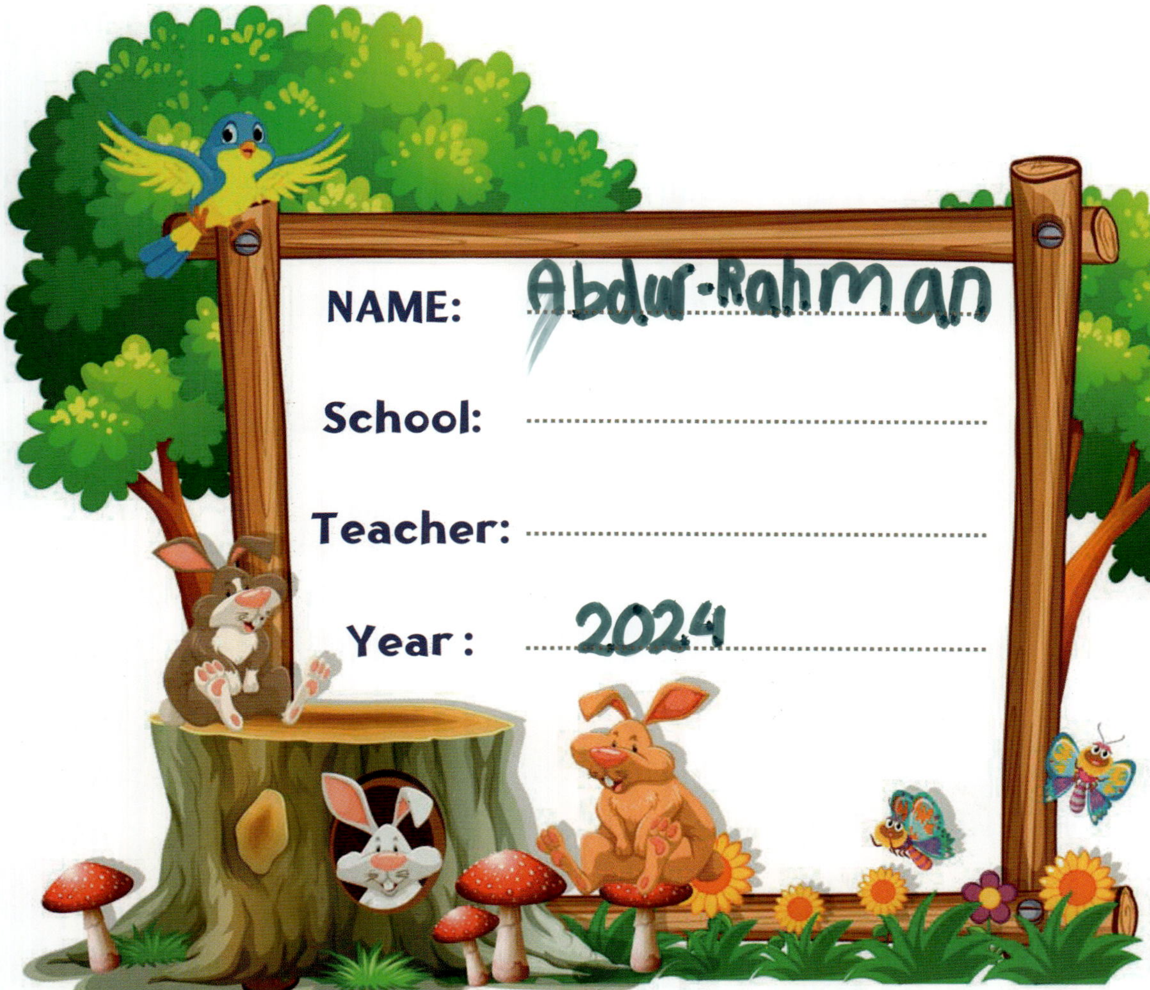

NAME: Abdur-Rahman

School: ....

Teacher: ....

Year : 2024

OUR BELIEF JOURNEY

1

INTRODUCTION

2

WORSHIP "IBADAH" 12

3

IBADAH EXERCISES 54

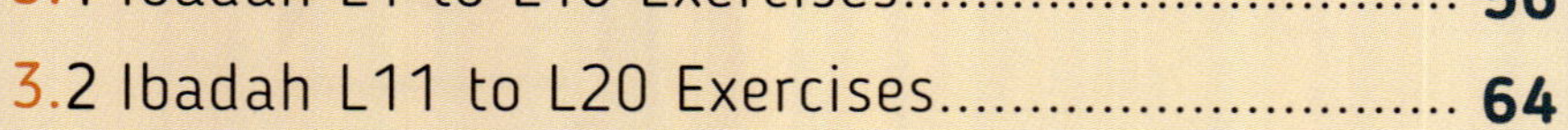

MANNERS "AKHLAQ" 72

AKHLAQ EXERCISES 122

WE BELIEVE

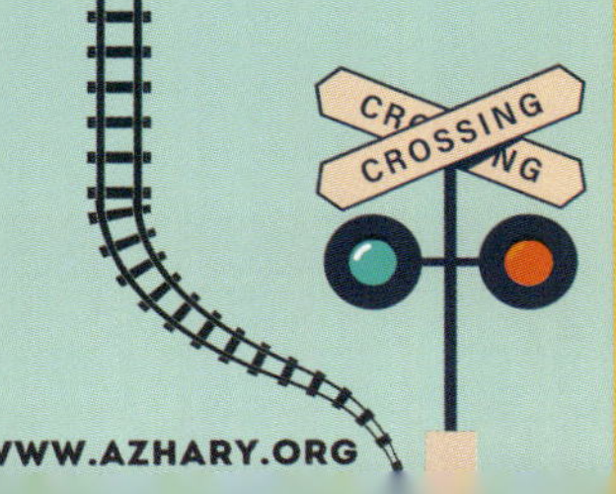

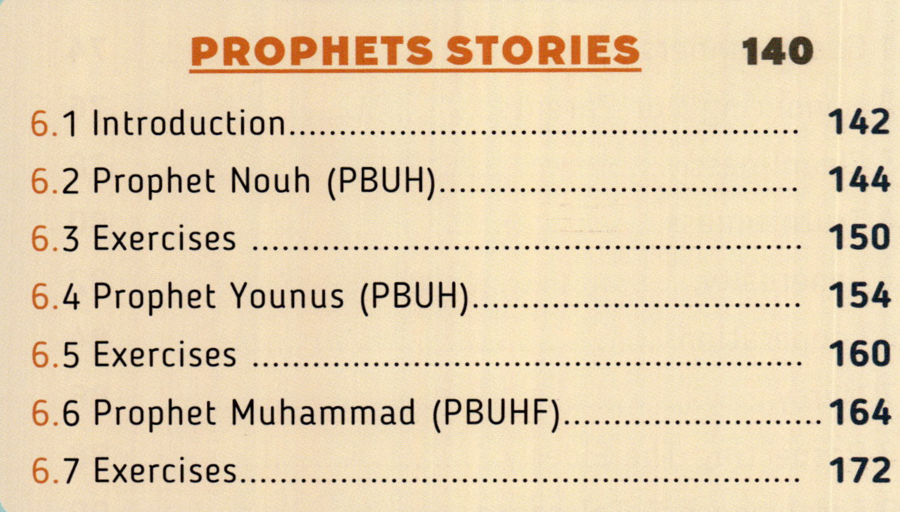

6 PROPHETS STORIES 140

7 EXAMS ISLAND 176

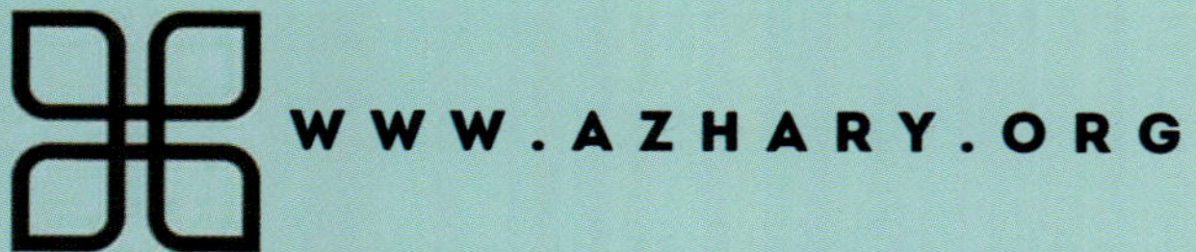

A LETTER TO OUR FUTURE

Assalamu Alaykum Wa Rahmatullahi Wa Barakatuh
(Peace, mercy, and blessings of Allah be upon you)

Dear young learners,
Did you know that Prophet Muhammad (PBUHF)* spent his entire life teaching others about Islam? We believe it's our responsibility to keep this message alive, just like a precious treasure passed down through generations.

That's why we created "We Believe," a special series of books for amazing kids like you! You are the future of Islam, and we want to make your learning journey about Allah exciting and fun.

Learning about Islam and sharing it with others is one of the most honourable things you can do. As you explore these books, you'll be taking a giant leap on this incredible path!

Remember, just like we're passing on the message to you, you'll get the chance to share it with others as you learn more. We pray that Allah blesses your learning journey and keeps you and your families happy and healthy wherever you are in the world.

We can't wait to see you grow in your faith!
With love and warm wishes,
The "We Believe" Team

*Peace Be Upon Him and his Family

بسم الله الرحمن الرحيم

ALL PRAISE IS DUE TO ALLAH; AND BLESSINGS AND PEACE BE UPON HIS MESSANGER AND SERVANT, MUHAMMAD, AND UPON HIS FAMILY, COMPANIONS, AND WHOEVER FOLLOWS HIS GUIDANCE UNTIL THE DAY OF RESURRECTION.

"WE BELIEVE"

NURTURING FAITH AND KNOWLEDGE FOR YOUNG MINDS

Welcome to the transformative world of "We Believe," a ground-breaking 14-volume series meticulously crafted to revolutionise Islamic education. Unlike any other program, "We Believe" ignites the flames of knowledge, equipping our future generation with the essential tools to confidently navigate the challenges of the 21st century.

But this endeavour is more than mere books; it's a movement. We break free from traditional, stagnant methods, embracing innovation and inclusivity. Our vision? A future where every Muslim child gains access to compelling, age-appropriate resources that fortify their faith and kindle their intellectual curiosity.

KEY FEATURES OF "WE BELIEVE":

- **Comprehensive Coverage:** Our third book delves into the rich tapestry of Islamic knowledge, seamlessly integrating Qur'an, Hadeeth, Aqeedah, Fiqh, and Seerah.
- **Structured Learning:** Explore three main sections:
  Ibadah (worship), Manners, and captivating Prophets' Stories.
- **Language Elevation:** Recognizing the power of words, we meticulously choose language structures that elevate students' eloquence. Our goal? To equip them with the precise terminology essential for their journey.
- **Arabic Treasure:** Dive into the (Arabic Treasure) section at the end of the lesson. Here, students engage in language learning, reinforced by online games and flashcards.
- **Testing and Reinforcement:** Various exercises follow each section, culminating in two comprehensive exams at the book's conclusion.
- **Beyond the Book:** Our commitment extends beyond the printed page. Online resources empower teachers, parents, and students alike.

ADDITIONAL FEATURES:

- **Dynamic QR Codes:** Each lesson includes a QR code granting access to teacher and parent guides, extra activities for both school and home use, revision notes, and mock tests. Just point your device's camera at the QR code, and a wealth of resources awaits you. Our commitment to continuous development ensures that these QR codes grant full access to our ever-evolving resources.
- **Comprehensive Curriculum:** Our journey involved scouring libraries, diving into the depths of knowledge, and sailing between the folds of books. We've brought forth treasures to create a curriculum to raise polymaths in Islamic Studies—a blend of deep-rooted tradition and modernity.
- **Addressing Misunderstanding:** Islam's misunderstanding by its followers has had catastrophic consequences within Muslim communities.
  Our curriculum seeks to offer blessed relief amidst lasting grief.
- **Authentic Sources:** Our school of thought rests upon Allah's Book and the authentic traditions of His last Prophet and Messenger (PBUHF)*. References to Qur'an verses and Hadeeths encourage critical thinking and authentic knowledge-seeking.

Age Range: Designed for ages 5 to 18, with additional resources tailored for pre-schoolers aged 3 and 4 through two specialised books.

Authored and Edited by Renowned Scholars: Our team comprises world-renowned scholars who graduated from Al-Azhar University in Egypt and conducted research at top universities in the US and Europe. They seamlessly blend authentic knowledge from its original sources with their deep understanding of Western societies and their unique challenges.

The result? A matchless learning experience for our youth.

JOIN US IN SHAPING A FUTURE WHERE KNOWLEDGE AND FAITH INTERTWINE SEAMLESSLY, NURTURING YOUNG HEARTS AND MINDS. "WE BELIEVE" IS NOT JUST A SERIES. IT IS A BEACON GUIDING OUR CHILDREN TOWARD ENLIGHTENMENT.

Feel free to explore this transformative journey with us!

*Peace Be Upon Him and his Family

OUR MAP TO YOUR BELIEF JOURNEY

Dear esteemed teachers, parents, and students,

We present you with a compass for navigating our book and maximizing the benefits of your learning and teaching journey. We proudly introduce We Believe Book 3, which comprises 7 distinct stations:

Introduction (1st Station)

Here, you'll prepare your gear for the exciting trip ahead. Receive your compass, map, and all the necessary equipment for a safe journey. Pay close attention to the instructions provided!

Ibadah (2nd Station)

Embark on a spiritual journey that covers 20 significant landmarks. Explore the pillars of Islam, the pillars of Eiman, and other essential concepts. Dive into the foundation of our religion and gain insights into crucial terminology. Learn how to perform Wudu' (ablution) and Salah (prayer), and contemplate profound ideas like destiny.

Ibadah Exercises (3rd Station)

Upon arrival, utilize your device's camera to scan the QR codes placed at the station's entrance. These codes grant access to revision notes and interactive quizzes. After refreshing yourself, prepare to navigate 16 engaging stops filled with fun activities. Beware of the Word-Search challenge—it's not for the faint-hearted!

Akhlaq (4th Station)

Your journey through good manners begins smoothly with 12 stops. However, brace yourself for a rocky stretch of 6 stops dedicated to bad manners. Fortunately, the path becomes smooth again in the final 6 stops before you reach the next station. Remember, our manners define us, so behave well, or you might face fines!

Akhlaq Exercises (5th Station)

We recognize that you've just completed a long journey of 24 stops, so take your time to rest in our Revision Hall. Recharge and prepare for the upcoming 16 stops filled with enjoyable activities. And yes, we won't mention the Word-Search warning again—consider yourself reminded!

Prophet Stories (6th Station)

Your train now splits through the beautiful dunes of sands in the Arabian Peninsula, embarking on an extraordinary exploration of sacred sites related to our beloved prophets:

Prophet Nouh's Ark and Mount Judi

Pause at this station to reflect on the story of Prophet Nouh and his remarkable ark. Imagine the vastness of the floodwaters and the belief that guided him.

Prophet Younus's All-Believers Village in Iraq

His resilience and trust in Allah are timeless inspirations. Witness the awe-inspiring moment when Prophet Younus was swallowed by a whale and then released. Rest on Pumpkin Island, where tranquillity meets divine intervention.

Mountains of Saudi Arabia (Makkah)

Brace yourself for a hilly ride as you approach Makkah. Here, you'll visit the sacred house of Allah (Ka'bah). If it's the blessed month of Dhul-Hijjah, consider yourself fortunate! Congrats on your Hajj!

Hira' and Thawr Caves

Explore the caves where our beloved Prophet Muhammad (peace and blessings be upon him) sought solitude and received divine revelations. Feel the weight of history and spirituality.

Journey to Madinah

Follow Prophet Muhammad (PBUHF)* as you travel to Madinah. Experience the serenity of this blessed city and take a well-deserved break in Yathrib.

Azhary Exam Island (7th Station)

Every journey, no matter how long, eventually reaches its destination. You've arrived at Azhary Exam Island—the final station of your 3rd First-Class We Believe Journey aboard the Azhary Press Train. Here, you'll showcase all the wonderful knowledge you've acquired, organise the landmarks you've visited, and celebrate your exploration.

Remember, this isn't a goodbye; it's a "see you again" as we eagerly await your participation in our 4th We Believe Journey. Thank you for being part of this enriching experience!

Warm regards. **Azhary Organisation**

*Peace Be Upon Him and his Family

WORSHIP

العِبَادَة

WORSHIP "IBADAH" 12

IBADAH EXERCISES 54

Al-ISLAM

Lesson objectives

- To define Islam.
- To learn the pillars of Islam.
- To discuss key points about Islam.

Islam: The last message Allah sent. It means submission: obeying Allah's commands.

Islam is the message Allah sent to Prophet Muhammad (PBUHF)* to be the seal of all messages. Allah won't accept any religion from us other than Islam.

To be a true Muslim, you must observe the following five pillars of Islam:

The Prophet (PBUHF) said:

"Verily, Al-Islam is founded on five (pillars): testifying the fact that there is no god but Allah, establishment of prayer, payment of Zakah, fast of Ramadan and Pilgrimage to the House (Ka'bah)."

(Al-Bukhari & Muslim)

*Peace Be Upon Him and his Family

We Believe

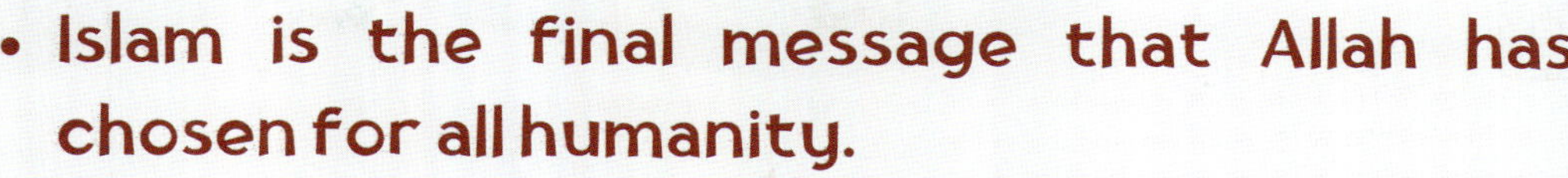

- Islam is the final message that Allah has chosen for all humanity.
- The religion of Islam is the straight path that leads to success.
- All the messengers submitted to Allah and worshiped Him sincerely.
- Islam is the greatest and most noble of Allah's blessings upon man, and through Islam, we will enter Paradise.
- Islam is a religion of ease, and its rulings and teachings are in line with human nature.
- To achieve Islam, you bear witness that there is no god but Allah and that Muhammad is His servant and Messenger.

DID YOU KNOW?

That 20% of the world's population are Muslims (around 2 billion people)!

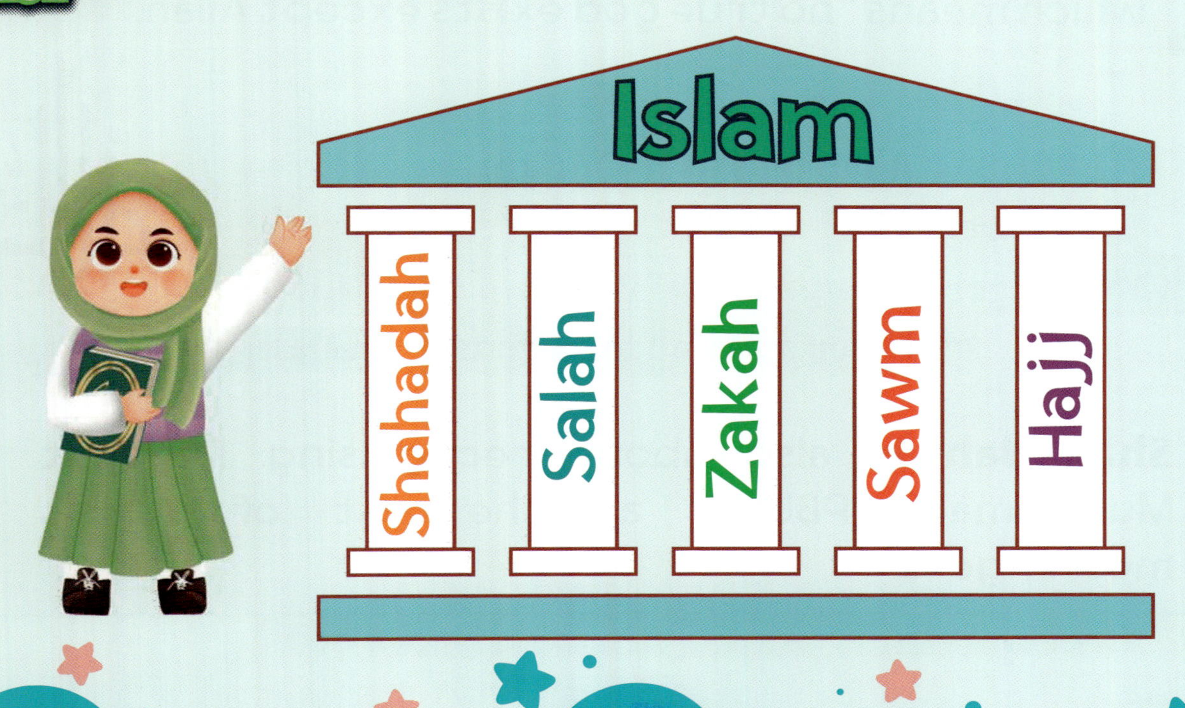

Shahadah

Lesson objectives

- To understand Allah's oneness.
- To realise the importance of Shahadah.
- To understand the significance of Prophethood.

Shahadah: an Arabic word that means witnessing/testifying.

THE MESSAGE OF ALL MESSENGERS

Shahadah is the first and the most important pillar of Islam. It is about **Tawheed:** the Oneness of Allah, which means "no true god exists except Allah.

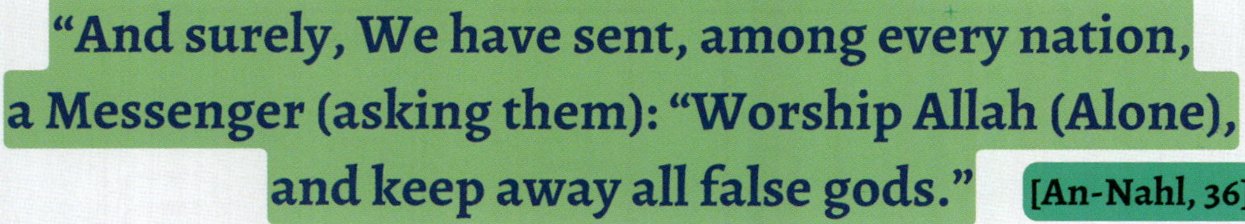

Allah tells us in Qur'an:

"And surely, We have sent, among every nation, a Messenger (asking them): "Worship Allah (Alone), and keep away all false gods." [An-Nahl, 36]

Shahadah is also about recognising Prophet Muhammad (PBUHF) as the last of Allah's messengers.

I WITNESS THAT THERE IS NO GOD BUT ALLAH.

I WITNESS THAT MUHAMMAD IS HIS LAST MESSENGER.

We Believe

- Allah created all things.
- Allah does not need help or assistance over creation.
- Allah is the only true god. He wasn't born and doesn't have a wife or children.

All of Allah's messages were about worshipping no god but Allah.

- Allah sent many messengers and prophets. We don't know their exact number.
- Prophet Muhammad is the seal "last" of all prophets and messengers.

Salah

Lesson objectives

- To realise the importance of Salah in Islam.
- To understand why we need to pray.

Salah: an Arabic word that means praying. It is the 2nd pillar of Islam.

A BELIEVER'S SHIELD

Salah is a connection you build with your Lord; you praise Him, glorify Him, and seek help from Him. Maintaining this connection keeps you alert to what is good and what is bad.

Allah tells us in Qur'an:

"Establish prayer. Indeed, ⌜genuine⌝ prayer should protect ⌜one⌝ from indecency and bad actions."

[Al-'Ankaboot, 45]

Salah is your shield, and it is your five daily reminders of your duty towards Allah. Whenever you need something, resort to Salah because it is the link between us and Allah that is never broken.

العِشاء
Isha'

The Prophet (PBUHF) informed us that Salah is the key to success in 'Akhirah "life after death".

He (PBUHF) also said:

"Indeed, the first deed by which a servant will be called to account on the Day of Resurrection is his Salah. If Salah is complete, he is successful and saved, but if it is defective, he has failed and lost."

(At- Tirmidhi)

Hence, we must take care of offering the five daily prayers at their prescribed times.

- Prayers should be performed as early as possible, and Salah should be a part of our daily activities.
- Salah is the **backbone** of Islam, and it is Allah's right upon us. It is for our benefit, and it is the best way to remember our Lord.

DID YOU KNOW

Humans and long-necked giraffes have the same number (7) of neck bones! Our backbone is 33 bones in total.

Wudu'

Lesson objectives

- To understand the meaning of Wudu'
- To know the etiquette of Wudu'.
- To learn how to perform Wudu'.
- To memorise the Du'a of Wudu'.

Wudu': an Arabic word that means beauty, brightness and cleanliness.

A BELIEVER'S BRIGHTNESS

Wudu' (Ablution) is one of the forms of cleanliness in Islam. It is done in a specific way and order. Muslims must have Wudu' before they pray.

Muslims should remain pure, and it is recommended to make Wudu' whenever they use the toilet, need to recite the Qur'an and when they are about to sleep.

Allah tells us in Qur'an:
"And Allah loves those who purify themselves." [At-Tawbahah,108]

WUDU' ETIQUETTE

Don't speak unless necessary!

Don't wet the area around you!

Don't waste water!

1 Wash your hands 3 times.

2 Rinse your mouth & nose 3 times.

3 Wash your face 3 times.

4 Wash your arms to elbow 3 times.

Start with your right arm!

5 Wipe your hair & ears once.

6 Wash your feet 3 times.

Start with your right foot!

Prophet Muhammad taught us to say this Du'a after Wudu':

(I bear witness that there is no god but Allah alone, with no partner, and I bear witness that Muhammad is His servant and His Messenger)

(أَشْهَدُ أَن لَّا إِلَهَ إِلَّا اللَّهُ وَحْدَهُ لَا شَرِيكَ لَهُ وَأَشْهَدُ أَنَّ مُحَمَّدًا عَبْدُهُ وَرَسُولُهُ)

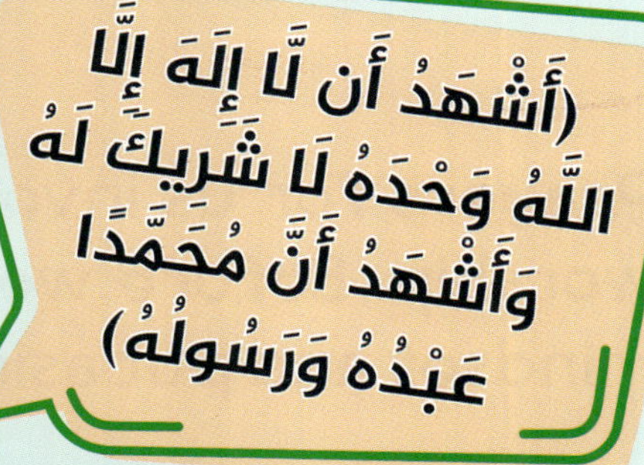

"O Allah, make me among those who repent and make me among those who are purified."

"اللَّهُمَّ اجْعَلْنِي مِنَ التَّوَّابِينَ وَاجْعَلْنِي مِنَ الْمُتَطَهِّرِينَ"

The Five Daily Prayers

Lesson objectives

- To learn the five daily prayers' history.
- To memorise their names in order.
- To design a prayer timetable.

THANK YOU, MY LORD!

Muslims pray five times daily because Allah Almighty has made it (Fard) obligatory.

Allah tells us in Qur'an:

"Indeed, Salah is obligatory on you according to its times." [An- Nisa', 103]

In the era of Prophet Mousa (PBUH), Salah was 50 times daily, but Allah, with His mercy, made it only 5 for us, the nation of Prophet Muhammad (PBUHF). Salah was made obligatory during the journey of Al- Isra' and Al- Mi'raj.

Prayers for us involve uniting mind, soul, and body in worship. Before we pray, we have to be in the right mindset and put aside all thoughts and worries.

Allah tells us in Qur'an:

"Successful indeed are the believers. Those who have their soul and mind in the prayer" [Al-Mu'minoon, 1-2]

Our prayers are for Allah and Allah only.

Fajr is a 2 Rak'ah Prayer at dawn. Qur'an is read loudly during Fajr.

الظُّهر
Dhuhr

Dhuhr is a 4 Rak'ah Prayer at noon. Qur'an is read silently in Dhuhr .

Asr is a 4 Rak'ah Prayer in the late afternoon. It is a silent prayer.

المَغْرِب
Maghrib

Maghrib is a 3 Rak'ah Prayer after sunset. It is a loud prayer.

Isha' is a 4 Rak'ah Prayer in the night. It is a loud prayer.

Activity

Design a prayer timetable for Azhary Grand Mosque!

Send your design via email to info@azhary.org for a chance to win a prize.

DID YOU KNOW?

The five daily prayers were originally 50, but after the Prophet (PBUHF) asked Allah, they got reduced to 5, and you still get rewarded for 50.

How to Pray?

Lesson objectives

- To learn how to perform Salah.
- To memorise what to say after each movement.

LET'S PRAY!

1

Face the Qiblah, raise your hands to your ears & say: Allahu Akbar.

2

Read Surat Al-Fatihah & any other Quranic verses.

3

Raise your hands saying: Allahu Akbar, then bow down for Rukou'.

4

During your Rukou', say: Subhana Rabbeya Al-Adheem (3 times).

5

Stand up saying: "Sami' Allahu Liman Hamidah" & "Rabbana Walakal Hamd"

6

Bow down and say: Subhana Rabbeya Al-A'la (3 times) during your Sujood.

Rise from Sujood and say: "Rabbi Ighfir Lee" before doing a second Sujood

Bow down and say: Subhana Rabbeya Al-A'la (3 times) during your Sujood.

When you finish the 2nd Sujood, you can either:

TASHAHUD التَّشَهُّد

ٱلتَّحِيَّاتُ لِلَّهِ وَٱلصَّلَوَاتُ وَٱلطَّيِّبَاتُ، ٱلسَّلَامُ عَلَيْكَ أَيُّهَا ٱلنَّبِيُّ وَرَحْمَةُ ٱللَّهِ وَبَرَكَاتُهُ، ٱلسَّلَامُ عَلَيْنَا وَعَلَى عِبَادِ ٱللَّهِ ٱلصَّالِحِينَ، أَشْهَدُ أَنْ لَا إِلَٰهَ إِلَّا ٱللَّهُ، وَأَشْهَدُ أَنَّ مُحَمَّدًا عَبْدُهُ وَرَسُولُهُ

At-Tahyatu Lillahi Wa Salawatu Wa Tayyibat. Assalamu Alayka Ayyuha Nabiyyu Wa Rahmatullahi Wa Barakatuh. Assalamu Alayna Wa Ala IbadiLlahi Saliheen. Ash-hadu Al-la Ilaha Ila Allah-u Wa Ash-hadu Anna Muhammadan Abduhu Wa Rasuluh.

9

اللَّهُمَّ صَلِّ عَلَى مُحَمَّدٍ وَعَلَى آلِ مُحَمَّدٍ كَمَا صَلَّيْتَ عَلَى إِبْرَاهِيمَ وَعَلَى آلِ إِبْرَاهِيمَ إِنَّكَ حَمِيدٌ مَجِيدٌ، اللَّهُمَّ بَارِكْ عَلَى مُحَمَّدٍ وَعَلَى آلِ مُحَمَّدٍ كَمَا بَارَكْتَ عَلَى إِبْرَاهِيمَ وَعَلَى آلِ إِبْرَاهِيمَ إِنَّكَ حَمِيدٌ مَجِيدٌ

Allahumma Salli 'Ala Muhammadin Wa Ala Aali Muhammadin Kama Sallayta Ala Ibraheem Wa Ala Aali Ibraheem Innaka Hameedun Majeed. Allahumma Baarik Ala Muhammadin Wa 'Ala Aali Muhammadin Kama Barakta Ala Ibraheem Wa 'Ala Aali Ibraheem Innaka Hameedun Majeed

Turn your head to the right saying: Assalamu Alaykum Wa Rahmatullah

10

Turn your head to the left saying: Assalamu Alaykum Wa Rahmatullah

DONE

Now you have finished and you can make Du'a and Dhikr.

Prayer Etiquette

Lesson objectives

- To define "Adab" etiquette.
- To learn prayer etiquette and how to behave in a mosque.

Adab: It is the polite behaviour people expect from you when you do something or deal with someone.

I'M RESPECTFUL

Allah is the most deserving of our respect. When it is prayer time, we should get ready for our Lord. We must understand that wherever we pray is sacred, and we should follow etiquette before, during and after our prayers.

BEFORE THE PRAYER

REMEMBER!

YOUR DU'A BEFORE ENTERING & LEAVING MASJID

Peace be upon the Messenger of Allah. Oh Allah, open for me the gates of Your mercy.

Peace be upon the Messenger of Allah. Oh Allah, I ask You from Your favour.

Zakah

Lesson objectives

- To learn the meaning of Zakah.
- To understand why we must give Zakah.
- To sow (the love of giving) value.
- To realise the impact of Zakah on society.

Zakah: an Arabic word that means purity. It is the 3rd pillar of Islam.

A BELIEVER'S PURITY

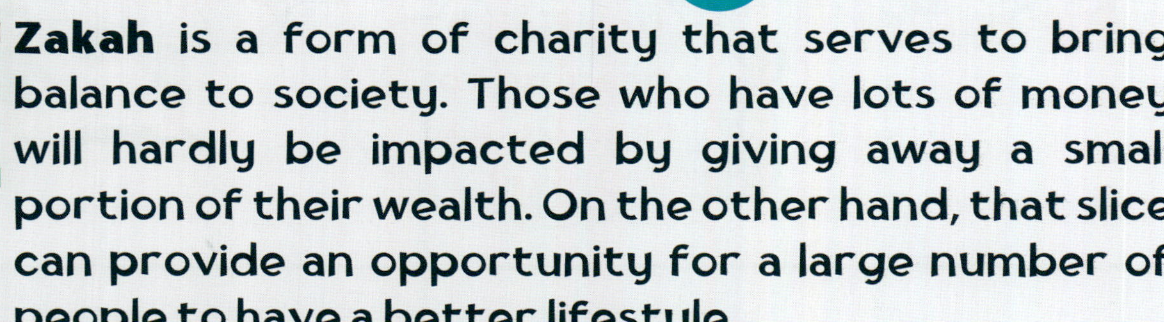

Zakah is a form of charity that serves to bring balance to society. Those who have lots of money will hardly be impacted by giving away a small portion of their wealth. On the other hand, that slice can provide an opportunity for a large number of people to have a better lifestyle.

Allah tells us in Qur'an:

"Take from their wealth ⌜O Prophet⌝ charity to purify and bless them." [At-Tawbah, 103]

Zakah is a part of our wealth that doesn't belong to us because Allah has already assigned it to the needy. Once we give that part to those who deserve it, our money becomes pure; **Zakah is purity**.

BEING MUSLIM... BEING GENTLE

We Believe that what we give to the needy is their right to our wealth. Allah praised us in Qur'an for fulfilling this duty:

> "and who give the rightful share of their wealth to the needy and the poor." [Al-Ma'arij, 24-25]

While giving Zakah, believers must be humble and should not have any pride, which can reduce their reward. It must be given respectfully, keeping others' feelings in mind.

We must be sensitive, and show compassion. We should be reminded that "**Kind words are better than charity followed by any harm.**"

We Believe

Rain is withheld from the sky when people hold back from giving Zakah and Allah would stop rain entirely if it weren't for animals.

REMEMBER!

Be grateful for what you have.
Know that Allah distributed our livelihood among us in this life, but His mercy is far better than any wealth we may have.

Lesson objectives

- To learn the meaning of Fasting.
- To understand the wisdom of Fasting.
- To realise the impact of Sawm on our manners.

Sawm: Arabic for giving up something for some time. It is the 4th pillar of Islam.

A BELIEVER'S STRENGTH

Sawm is to stop eating and drinking from dawn till sunset. Children don't need to fast, but they can try for a few hours as a taster.

You may be thinking, oh, this is hard! You are right. It is not an easy job. That is why we get to practise till we are old enough and ready to fast.

Allah addresses us in Qur'an:

"O believers! Fasting is prescribed for you—as it was for those before you—so perhaps you will become mindful ˹of Allah˺." [Al-Baqarah, 183]

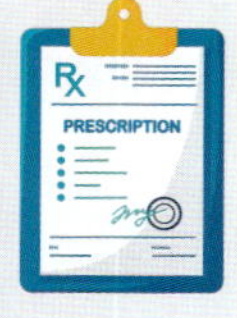

Fasting teaches us to be mindful of Allah and mindful of how it feels like to be starving. How it must feel for those who are unable to buy food to eat or find clean water to drink.

REWARD

The reward for fasting is so great that Allah left it to The Hereafter. It is very special!

Abu Umamah asked our Prophet (PBUHF):

" 'O Messenger of Allah, tell me of an action I should do.' He said, ' Take to fasting, for nothing is equal." (An-Nasa'i)

Ramadan

When fasting is mentioned, Ramadan is the first thing that comes to mind. It is a holy month for us; the month of Sawm and Qur'an.

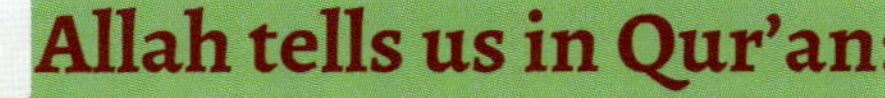

Allah tells us in Qur'an:

"Ramadan is the month in which the Qur'an was revealed... So whoever is present this month, let them fast..." [Al-Baqarah, 185]

You also get two pleasures: one when you break your fast and another when you meet your Lord.

Fasting teaches you to be strong and patient. It is an opportunity to break bad habits.

What are the bad habits you would like to give up?

You can discuss this with your teacher/parent!

Hajj

Lesson objectives

- To learn the meaning of Hajj.
- To examine equality in Islam.
- To plan the journey of a lifetime.

Hajj: (Pilgrimage) Arabic for a journey to a sacred place. It is the 5th & the last pillar of Islam.

A BELIEVER'S JOURNEY

Hajj is a religious journey every adult Muslim must make to the holy city of Makkah (Mecca) in Saudi Arabia. Every Muslim who is financially and physically able must make the pilgrimage at least once in a lifetime.

Allah tells us in Qur'an:

"Pilgrimage to this House is an obligation by Allah upon whoever is able among the people." ['Al-Imran, 97]

Hajj begins on the 8th day of Dhul-Hijjah (the last month of the Islamic year) and ends on the 13th day

Millions of pilgrims from all over the world gather in **Makkah** to go around **Ka'bah** and stand on **Arafat** Mountain. The rich and the poor, the black and the white, the king and the servant, all dressed the same and all humbled before their Lord.

It is an amazing scene of equality.

BORN AGAIN

The Prophet (PBUHF) informed us that the reward for an accepted Hajj is Jannah.

He (PBUHF) also said:

" Whoever performs Hajj for Allah and does not do evil or sins then they will return (after Hajj free from all sins) as if they were born anew."

What a wonderful chance! (Al-Bukhari & Muslim)

Al-Masjid Al-Haram in Makkah is the best place on earth you can ever visit. A trip there can help you be a better human being.

We ask Allah to grant you and your loved ones this wonderful trip.

Activity

Make a 5-point plan for your Hajj journey!

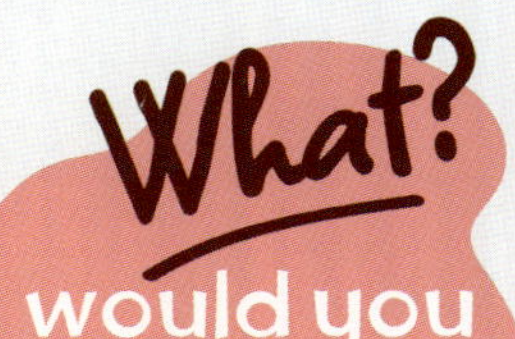

What? cities and places would you visit?

Go to pages 56-63 for exercises on Lessons 1-10.

Al-EIMAN

Lesson objectives

- To define Eiman.
- To learn the pillars of Eiman.
- To understand the difference between Eiman & Islam.

Eiman Arabic for Belief, and it is an act of the heart. Eiman is the key to a happy and peaceful life.

Eiman Pillars

Eiman was beautifully explained in detail when a man came to the Prophet (PBUHF) while he was sitting with his companions and asked him, "What is belief?"

The Prophet (PBUHF) replied:

"It is to believe in Allah, His angels, His Books, His Messengers and the Last Day and that you believe in destiny, its bad and good consequences." (Muslim)

Eiman is an act of the heart, and it is the gate to Jannah. In the hereafter, Allah will allow those who have even a tiny bit of Eiman to enter Jannah.

Oh Allah, give us a never changing strong belief in you!

THE RIGHT PATH

Eiman is the fuel that gives you the power to apply the pillars of Islam. It is the soul that keeps the body alive. **Eiman** comes first, and it opens the door to our beautiful religion.

Jundub Ibn Abdullah said:

"We were with the Prophet (ﷺ), and we were strong youths, so we learned faith before we learned Qur'an. (Ibn Majah)

- Allah looks at our hearts and knows how strong our belief in Him.
- The Pillars of Islam are physical acts, and Eiman is the engine to power these pillars.
- Eiman is the strongest tie we have to our Lord, and we must preserve it.

Oh Allah, endear faith to us; make it appealing in our hearts. And make us hate disbelief, rebelliousness, and disobedience.

Lesson objectives

- To know the meaning of the word Allah.
- To understand why Allah created us.
- To reflect on Allah's miracles of creation.

Allah: It is a special name for God and is given only to Him. It means the God whom we must worship alone and no one else.

WHY WERE WE CREATED?

FIRST 1

Allah created human beings and made them the greatest and most honourable creatures.
This honour comes with a responsibility: to build and establish a good life on earth. Also, to fulfil the main task we were created for and the right of Allah upon us.F

The Prophet “PBUHF said:

"Allah's Right upon His slaves is that they should worship Him Alone and associate nothing with Him.”

(Al-Bukhari & Muslim).

To believe in Allah, we have to understand who Allah is!

Allah sent us Qur'an to guide us. He told us how to worship Him and what to do or not to do.

Whenever you need to talk to Allah, you should pray and ask Him to grant you what is good for you in this life and the hereafter.

Allah tells us in Qur'an:

When My servants ask you ⌜O Prophet⌝ about Me: I am truly near. I respond to one's prayer when they call upon Me.

[Al-Baqarah, 186]

- Allah is one, and He has no parents, wife, and no children.
- Allah has no equal or likeness.
- Allah has 99 names, and whoever learns them will go to Jannah.
- Allah is always there for us whenever we need Him. We need to ask Him.

The word Allah has been mentioned in Qur'an "2557" times.

The Angels

Lesson objectives

- To understand the nature of angels.
- To learn angels' names and duties.
- To realise the importance of believing in angels.

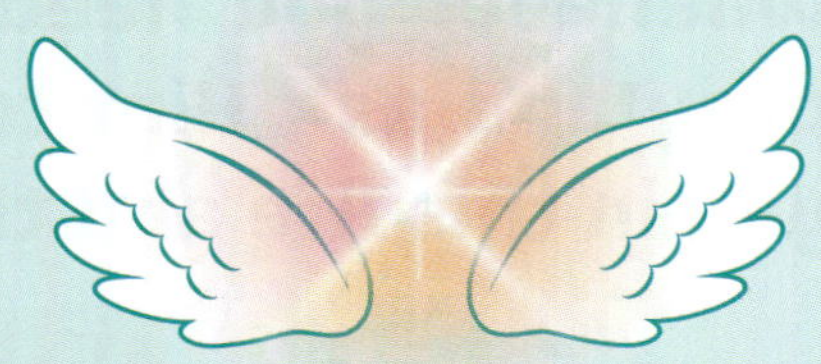

Angels: Angels are gentle, luminous bodies that humans cannot see. They listen to Allah and never disobey his commands.

ATTRIBUTES OF ANGELS

Allah created angels and gave them characteristics that distinguish them from humans:

- Allah created them from light.

The Prophet "PBUHF said:
"Angels were created from light." (Muslim)

- Allah created angels with wings.
- They neither eat nor drink.

Angels remember Allah and glorify Him day and night. They never get tired.

Allah created many angels, and they have different names and duties. We don't know the angels' exact number, except the ones Allah and His Prophet (PBUHF) told us about.

Israfeel

He blows the trumpet to signal the start of the Hereafter.

Meekal

He is the angel of rain and plants.

Jibreel

He is Allah's messenger angel sent to His messengers on earth.

Munkar and Nakeer

They test the faith of the dead in their graves.

Malik and Ridwan

Malik guards Hellfire & Ridwan guards Jannah

Allah also told us in Qur'an about many other angels without mentioning their names.

There is the angel of death and the angels who protect us. There are also "The Honorable Writers"; two angels with each person, one on the right writing the good deeds, and the one on the left writing the bad deeds.

- Believing in angels is the second pillar of Eiman.
- Angels love the believers. Angels also seek forgiveness for people who seek knowledge.
- Angels surround us when we recite Qur'an or study the teachings of Allah.

The Scriptures

Lesson objectives

- To learn about the main Books of Allah.
- To understand the purpose of scriptures.
- To learn the difference between Qur'an and the other books.

Scriptures: The sacred books that Allah sent to His messengers as guidance for their nations.

Az-Zabour

"**Az-Zabour**" or Psalms is the book that was sent to Prophet Dawoud "David" (PBUH).

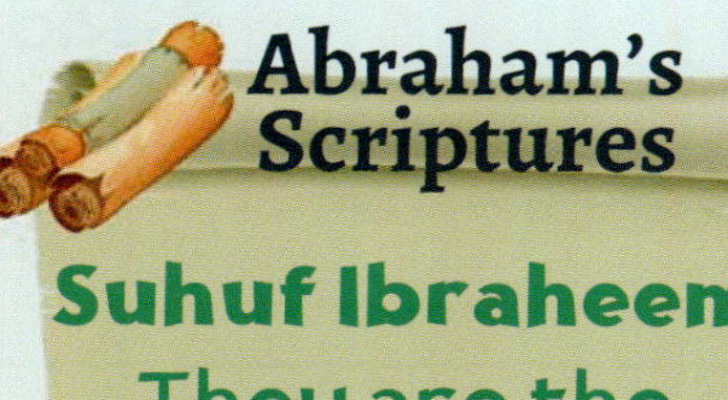

Abraham's Scriptures

Suhuf Ibraheem
They are the teachings sent to Prophet Ibraheem (PBUH).

The Torah

At-Tawrah;
Torah was sent to the prophet Mousa (PBUH) and it was the main book sent to the people of Israel.

The Bible

Al-Injeel
The Bible was sent to Prophet Eisa (PBUH) and it's a completion of the Torah.

The Holy Qur'an

Al-Qur'an is the last book of Allah. It was sent to His last prophet Muhammad (PBUHF) in Arabic.

THE MAIN MESSAGE

All the sacred books that Allah sent to His messengers had one main message: to worship Allah alone and no one else. The books also contained guidance to help people live a good and meaningful life.

Allah tells us in Qur'an:

"And We sent not before you any messenger except We revealed to him that, "There is no deity except Me, so worship Me." [Al-Anbiya', 25]

THE GREAT QUR'AN

What makes **Qur'an** different from the rest of the texts is that it was sent to Prophet Muhammad (PBUHF) in **Arabic**, and it is still written and recited in Arabic and will remain protected till the end of time.

Allah tells us in Qur'an:

"Indeed, it is We who sent down Qur'an, and indeed, We will be its guardian." [Al-Hijr, 9]

Activity

Match each Messenger with his Message.

- [ ] Al-Qur'an
- [ ] Az-Zabour
- [ ] Al-Injeel
- [ ] At-Tawrah
- [x] The Scriptures of Abraham

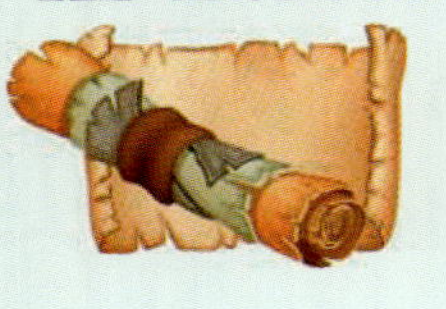

The Messengers

Lesson objectives

- To understand the mission of the messengers.
- To learn from their manners.
- To know our duty towards them.

Messengers: People chosen by Allah to guide their nations to worship Him alone, without partners.

THEIR MISSION

Allah sent His blessings on His creation when He sent among them messengers bringing good tidings and warnings, reciting the verses of their Lord, teaching them what would be best for them, and guiding them to the source of their happiness in this world and the hereafter.

Allah addresses us in Qur'an:

"Messengers who gave good news as well as warnings."

[An-Nisa', 165]

Out of Allah's mercy to His servants, He sent the messengers to be role models and good examples in obedience, worship, and morals.

- Muslims love all prophets and messengers and don't prefer some over others.
- We have to send peace and blessings upon them.
- We have to learn and spread the word of Allah as much as we can, like His Prophets.

DID YOU KNOW? The first messenger is Nouh(PBUH), and the last is Muhammad (PBUHF).

The Hereafter

Lesson objectives

- To learn what to believe about 'Akhirah.
- To understand accountability.
- To learn how to prepare for 'Akhirah.

Hereafter: After we die, Allah will bring us back to another life at the end of time to judge us on our actions during this life.

On that day, Allah will divide people based on their actions: **People of the Right** are the believers and **People of the Left** are the non-believers. We live our lives to prepare for real life in the Hereafter.

Allah tells us in Qur'an:

"This worldly life is no more than play and amusement. But the Hereafter is indeed the real life. If only they knew!"

[Al-'Ankaboot, 64]

THE JUDGMENT DAY

The People of the Left, if they never changed, will be punished by Allah for all the evil things they did and will go to Hellfire.

The People of the Right, as a reward for their deeds, will go to Jannah and enjoy a lasting life that no one could imagine.

How? to prepare for the hereafter?

Don't cause harm!

Be Caring!

Love Your Prophet!

Obey Allah!

Obey Your Parents!

Be Merciful!

Respect The Elderly!

Observe Salah!

Don't Lie!

- Allah loves us, and no matter what we do, He awaits us to seek His forgiveness.
- This life is a test, and Allah is watching to see who will be thankful and who won't.
- Our Prophet (PBUHF) will ask Allah to forgive us and will save so many in The Hereafter.

Arabic Treasure

HEREAFTER	آخِرَة
RIGHT	يَمِين
LEFT	شِمَال

Destiny

Lesson objectives

- To define (Qadar) destiny.
- To examine destiny in our lives.
- To understand the difference between free will and destiny.

In Islam, we believe that Allah has a special plan for everything that happens in our lives. This plan is called "Qadar".

WE TRUST IN ALLAH

Allah created us and gave us "Free Will"; the power to choose. Because Allah knows everything, He knows what we will do in this life and has already written it.

Our Prophet (PBUHF) said to Abdullah Ibn Abbas:
"Know that what you have failed to get was not meant to happen for you, and what has happened to you was not going to pass you by". (At-Tirmidhi & Ahmed)

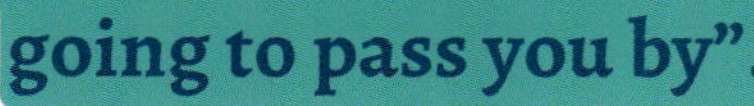

We plan, work hard and do what we can, knowing that the results are within the power of Allah. Whatever happens in the end, we accept and say (Al-Hamdulillah).

ALLAH KNOWS BEST

Allah is All-knowing, but our knowledge is limited. How many times have we thought that something is good, but it turned out to be bad for us and vice versa?

Allah tells us in Qur'an

"You may hate something which Allah turns into a great blessing." [An-Nisa', 19]

The Prophet (PBUHF) taught us: "If the whole world came together to benefit or harm you with anything, they would not be able to, except with what Allah had already decided for you."

We Believe

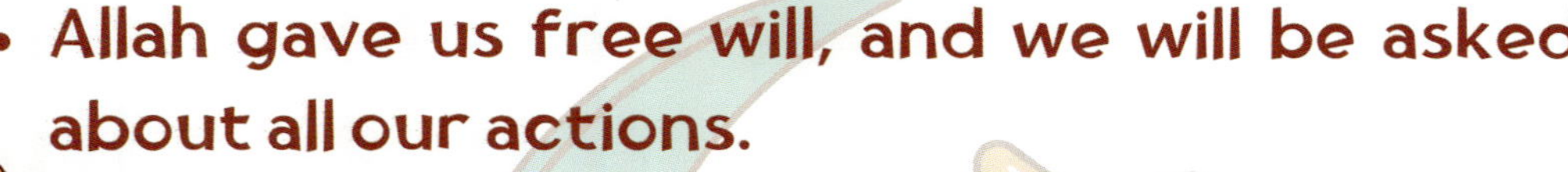

- Allah gave us free will, and we will be asked about all our actions.
- There are things that we can't have control or knowledge of. When and where we die, our future and the Hereafter.
- Everything happens for a reason, and it is all part of Allah's plan for us.
- We should do our part and trust in Allah's planning for us.

Eid-ul-Fitr

Lesson objectives

- To understand Eid-ul-Fitr's meaning.
- To learn Eid acts of Sunnah.
- To discuss and share what we do during Eid.

Eid-ul-Fitr is a 1-day celebration of breaking fast after Ramadan. Muslims worldwide celebrate it on the **1st of Shawwal** (Hijri Calendar).

1 Muslims start Eid day by eating something sweet to mark the end of Ramadan.

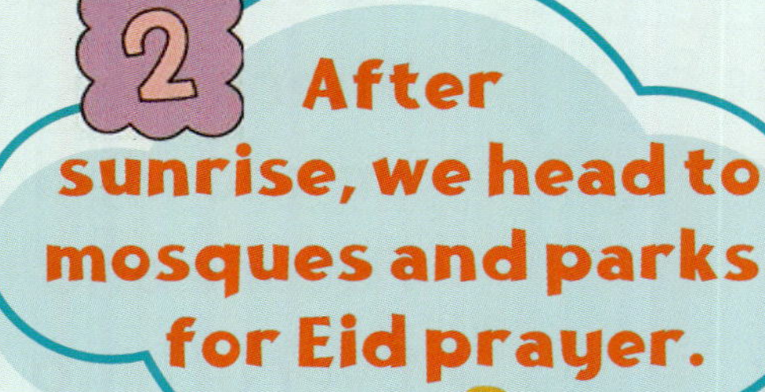

2 After sunrise, we head to mosques and parks for Eid prayer.

JOY

3 Families get together to have a meal, and the kids play and enjoy their time.

EID ACTS OF SUNNAH

Take a shower!

Eat Breakfast!

Wear the best clothes!

Wear Perfume!

Say Eid Takbeerat!

Walk to the mosque.

Pray Eid in a congregation!

Connect with family and friends!

Exchange gifts!

Eid-ul-Adha

Lesson objectives

- To understand the meaning of Eid.
- To know how we celebrate Eid-ul-Adha.
- To learn the Prophet's Sunnah in Eid.

Eid is a festival and Al-Adha is sacrifice. Muslims around the world celebrate Eid-ul-Adha on the 10th of Dhul-Hijjah (Hijri Calendar).

HAPPY EID

During the month of Dhul-Hijjah, millions of Muslims worldwide travel to Makkah in Saudi Arabia to perform Hajj and fulfil the fifth pillar of Islam.

Take a shower and wear your nicest clothes.

Go with family & friends to the Eid prayer.

After Salah, greet people you meet.

Eat from your Qurbani & Enjoy Your Eid!

TAKBEER IN EID DAYS

اللهُ أَكْبَرُ — اللهُ أَكْبَرُ — اللهُ أَكْبَرُ

لَا إِلَهَ إِلَّا اللهُ

It is a Sunnah to praise Allah by saying the Takbeer during Eid-ul-Adha days.

اللهُ أَكْبَرُ — اللهُ أَكْبَرُ — وَلِلَّهِ ٱلْحَمْدُ

After Eid prayer, Muslims distribute the Qurbani "Ud-heyah" meat to family, friends, neighbours, and the needy.

Allah tells us in Qur'an:

So eat of it (Qurbani) and feed the miserable and poor.

[Al-Hajj, 28]

During Eid days, we should visit our neighbours, family and friends. We share food, exchange gifts, and bring joy and happiness.

REMEMBER!

As Muslims, we have to be mindful of those around us during times of celebration. For example, we shouldn't block roads or disturb our neighbours.

Du'a In Our Life

Lesson objectives

- To learn the importance of Du'a.
- To memorise some essential Du'a.
- To understand that Du'a is a way of life.

Du'a: It is a conversation with Allah in which we place our needs before Him and ask for His help in solving our problems.

Allah is the one who protects us from all evil. Our Du'a is how we connect with Him and ask for help and guidance. We trust that Allah will always be there for us.

WEARING CLOTHES DU'A

الْحَمْدُ لِلَّهِ الَّذِي
كَسَانِي هَذَا، وَرَزَقَنِيهِ
مِنْ غَيْرِ حَوْلٍ مِنِّي،
وَلَا قُوَّةٍ

Praise is to Allah Who has clothed me with this (garment) and provided it for me, though I was powerless myself and incapable

LEAVING THE HOUSE DU'A

بِسْمِ اللَّهِ تَوَكَّلْتُ
عَلَى اللَّهِ، وَلَا حَوْلَ
وَلَا قُوَّةَ إِلَّا بِاللَّهِ.

In the name of Allah, I place my trust in Allah, and there is no might nor power except with Allah.

BEFORE STUDYING

رَبِّ اشْرَحْ لِي صَدْرِي
وَيَسِّرْ لِي أَمْرِي وَاحْلُلْ
عُقْدَةً مِّن لِّسَانِي
يَفْقَهُوا قَوْلِي.

"O my Lord! Open up my heart and make my task easy for me, and loosen the knot from my tongue so that they might fully understand my speech."

TRAVELLING DU'A

سُبْحَانَ الَّذِي سَخَّرَ لَنَا
هَذَا وَمَا كُنَّا لَهُ
مُقْرِنِينَ. وَإِنَّا إِلَى رَبِّنَا
لَمُنقَلِبُونَ.

Glory is to Him Who has provided this for us though we could never have had it by our efforts.

ENTERING THE TOILET

(بِسْمِ اللَّه) اللَّهُمَّ
إِنِّي أَعُوذُ بِكَ مِنَ
الْخُبْثِ وَالْخَبائِثِ

[In the Name of Allah]. O Allah, I seek protection in You from evil and the evil ones.

DID YOU KNOW?

Du'a is the best act a Muslim can do to worship Allah.

Go to pages 64-71 for exercises on Lessons 11-22.

IBADAH

Scan QR code!

Lessons 1-10

Lessons 11-20

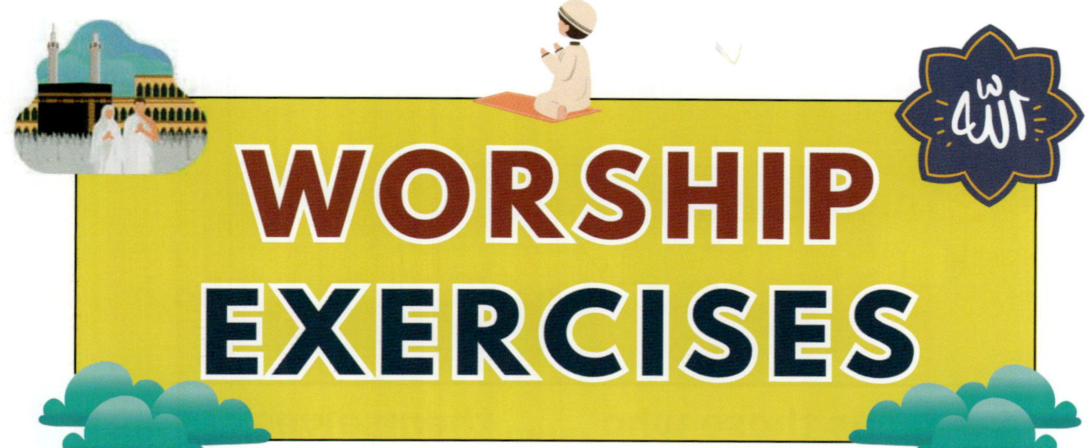

WORSHIP EXERCISES

For Revision Notes and Quizzes.

For Arabic Treasure Practice

AZHARY PRESS

Choose the correct answer!

EXERCISES

1 Islam is based on five ....

- [ ] houses
- [x] pillars
- [ ] companies

2 Allah doesn't have ....

- [ ] a son
- [x] a wife
- [ ] both

3 Allah loves those who .... themselves.

- [x] purify
- [ ] teach
- [ ] love

4 .... is the 3rd pillar of Islam.

- [ ] Shahadah
- [x] Zakah
- [ ] Hajj

5 Fasting teaches us to be ....

- [x] patient
- [ ] hungry
- [ ] thirsty

6 There are .... joys for those who fast.

- [ ] unlimited
- [x] five
- [ ] two

7 Hajj is a .... journey.

- [ ] historical
- [ ] educational
- [x] religious

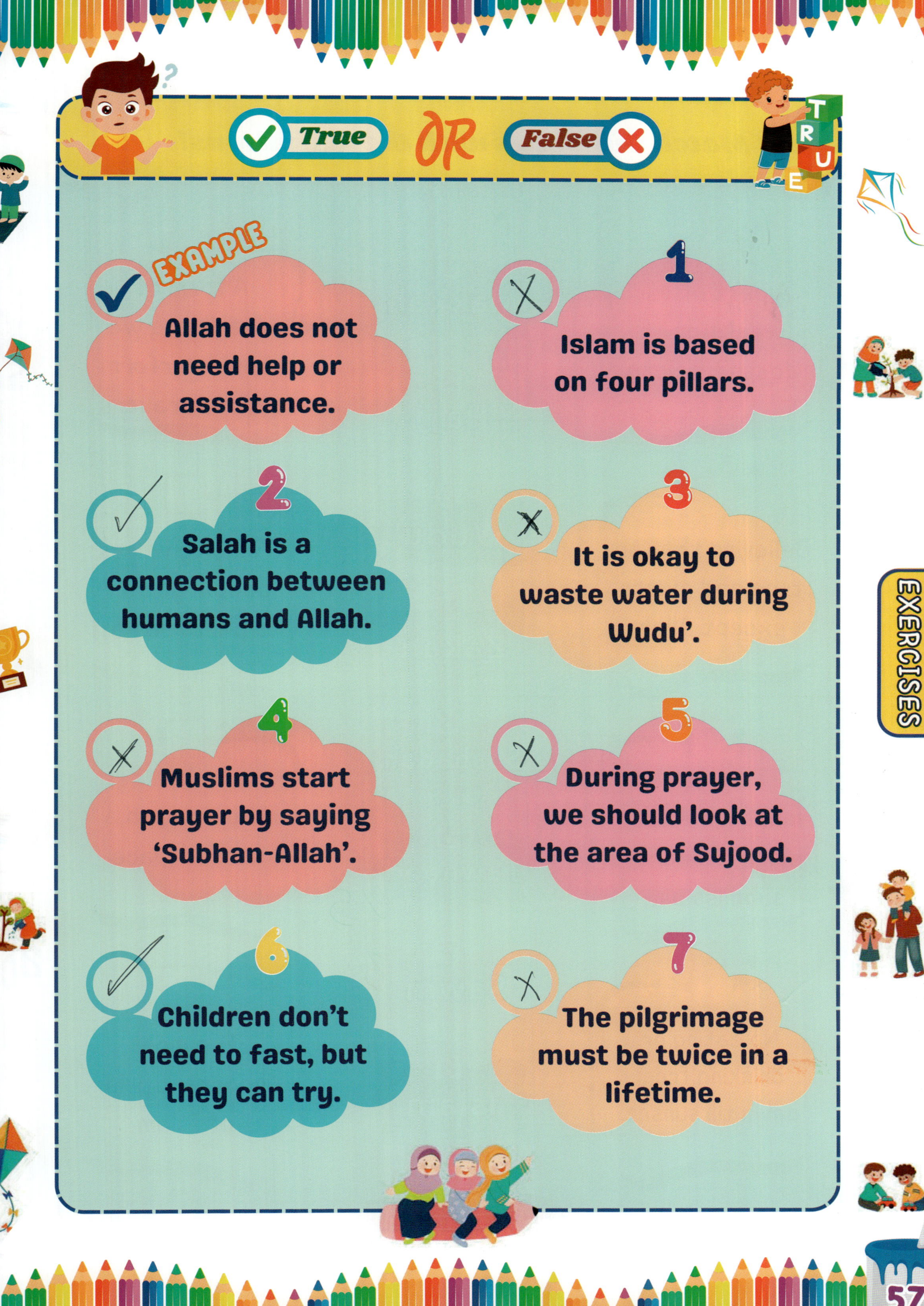
True
OR
False
T
R
U
E
EXAMPLE
Allah does not need help or assistance.
1
Islam is based on four pillars.
2
Salah is a connection between humans and Allah.
3
It is okay to waste water during Wudu'.
4
Muslims start prayer by saying 'Subhan-Allah'.
5
During prayer, we should look at the area of Sujood.
6
Children don't need to fast, but they can try.
7
The pilgrimage must be twice in a lifetime.
EXERCISES
57

Match the words with the definitions!

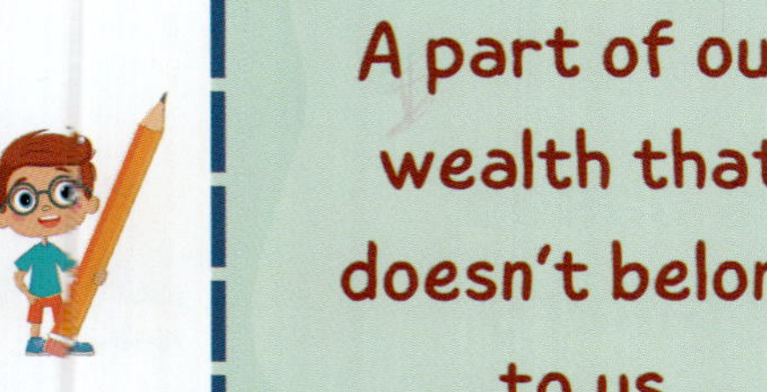

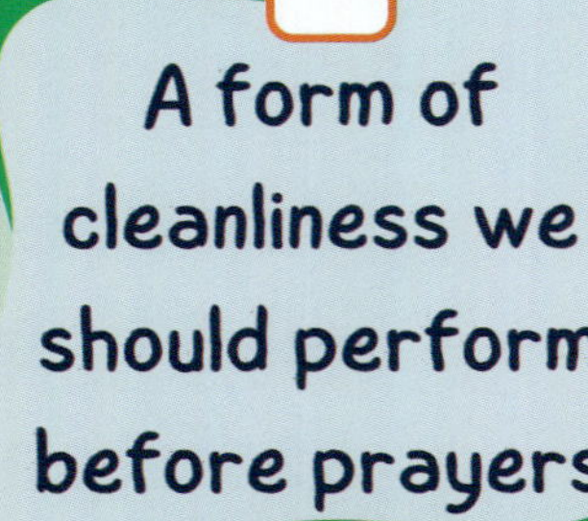

A part of our wealth that doesn't belong to us

A form of cleanliness we should perform before prayers

1. Makkah
2. Hajj
3. Wudu'
4. Zakah
5. Shahadah
6. Tawheed
7. Sawm
8. Islam

Believing that no true god exists except Allah

The city where people gather to perform Hajj

The last message Allah sent, it means submission.

A journey to a sacred place

No eating or drinking from dawn till sunset.

The most important pillar of Islam

EXERCISES

1. Sawm is to stop eating, but you can drink.

2. 10% of the world's population are Muslims.

3. Dhul-Hijjah is the last month of the Hijri year.

4. Muslims fast during the month of Shawwal.

5. We start Wudu' by washing our arms.

6. During prayer, we must read Surat Al-Fatihah each Rak'ah.

7. Shahadah is the second pillar of Islam.

8. Shahadah has 2 parts.

Rearrange Wudu' Steps!
Wash your arms 3 times.
Wash your feet 3 times.
Wash your face 3 times.
1
بِسْمِ اللهِ
Wash your hands 3 times.
Rinse your mouth & nose 3 times.
Wipe your hair & ears once.
EXERCISES
60

Match The Salah With Its Description!

Fajr

EXAMPLE

2 Rak'ah Prayer at dawn. Qur'an is read loudly during it.

Isqr

4 Rak'ah Prayer in the night. It is a loud prayer.

ASUR

4 Rak'ah Prayer at noon. Qur'an is read silently during it.

Magrihb.

3 Rak'ah Prayer after sunset. It is a loud prayer.

za'har.

4 Rak'ah Prayer in the late afternoon. It is a silent prayer.

EXERCISES

Match Arabic with English!

Arabic Treasure

English	Arabic	
1 Oneness	رُكْن	
2 Testimony	الْفُقَرَاء	
3 Hunger	صِيَام	
4 Prayer	تَوْحِيد	1
5 Fasting	رَسُول	
6 The poor	صَلَاة	
7 Charity	جُوع	
8 Pillar	شَهَادَة	
9 Messenger	زَكَاة	

Word Search Puzzle!

(Words can be found in any direction, including diagonal, and can overlap each other.)

M	E	S	S	E	N	G	E	R	G	Z	Y
A	N	U	F	I	S	R	D	M	P	F	N
L	A	J	E	W	A	A	H	S	I	U	H
L	B	O	I	M	D	H	W	G	H	K	A
A	M	O	A	H	A	A	Q	Y	S	F	D
H	U	D	X	L	P	J	B	C	R	H	A
F	A	M	A	Y	M	J	A	M	O	C	H
N	I	S	L	A	M	Q	S	H	W	F	A
B	A	B	M	A	G	H	R	I	B	A	H
G	O	O	D	C	H	I	L	D	Z	J	S
Y	M	O	S	Q	U	E	X	E	A	R	S
S	Q	J	K	P	U	R	I	T	Y	K	C

HAJJ	WORSHIP	SAWM	FAJR
EARS	ISLAM	SHAHADAH	ASR
MAGHRIB	ISHAA	SUJOOD	RAMADAN
ALLAH	MESSENGER	PURITY	MOSQUE

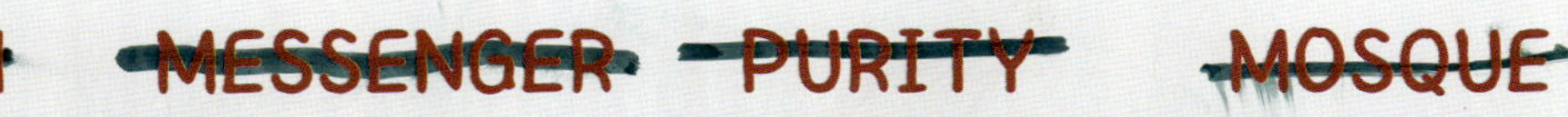

Choose the correct answer!

1. "Allah" is mentioned in Qur'an .... times.
   - [ ] 2557
   - [ ] 9867
   - [ ] 1259

2. Azzabour was sent to Prophet ....
   - [ ] Ibraheem
   - [ ] Mousa
   - [ ] Dawoud

3. During Hajj we stand on .... Mountain.
   - [ ] Arafat
   - [ ] Hira'
   - [ ] Uhud

4. .... is a pillar of Eiman.
   - [ ] Destiny
   - [ ] Sawm
   - [ ] Hajj

5. Allah created angels from ....
   - [ ] fire
   - [ ] clay
   - [ ] light

6. ....is the angel of rain and plants.
   - [ ] Jibreel
   - [ ] Meekal
   - [ ] Israfeel

7. The Torah was sent to Prophet ....
   - [ ] Ibraheem
   - [ ] Mousa
   - [ ] Dawoud

1. Eiman is an act of the body.

2. Qur'an can be recited in English.

3. Allah didn't give us the power to choose.

4. Angels were created from light, and they eat and drink.

5. Eid-ul-Adha comes during the month of Dhul-Hijjah.

6. The first thing we will be asked about in 'Akhirah is Sawm.

7. Qur'an was sent to Prophet Muhammad in Urdu.

8. Eid-ul-Fitr is right before Ramadan.

Match the words with the definitions!

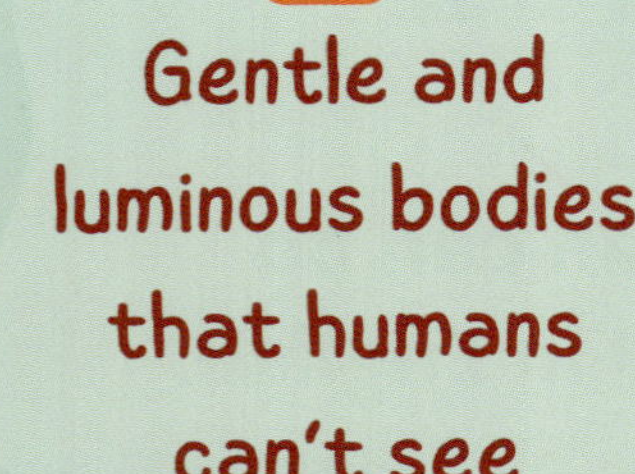

☐ Gentle and luminous bodies that humans can't see

☐ The sacred books that Allah sent to His messengers

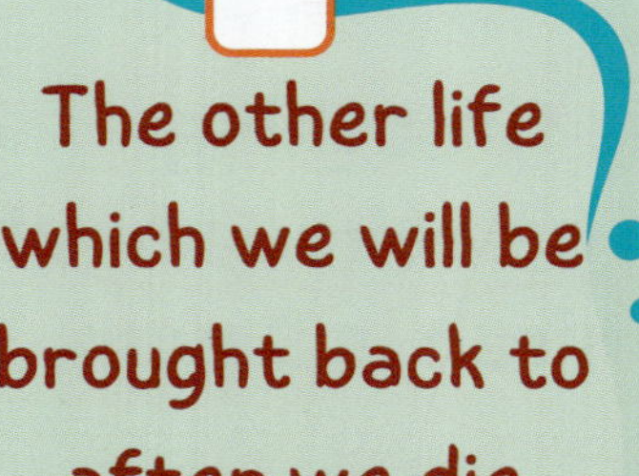

☐ The other life which we will be brought back to after we die

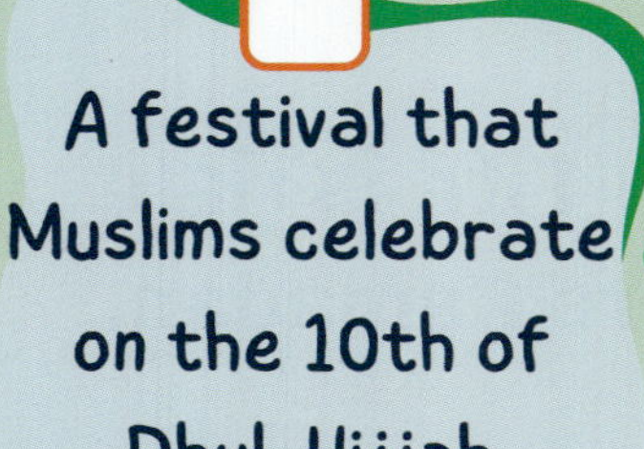

☐ A festival that Muslims celebrate on the 10th of Dhul-Hijjah

1 Messengers

2 Hereafter

3 Du'a

4 Eid-ul-Adha

5 Scriptures

6 Allah

7 Angels

8 Destiny

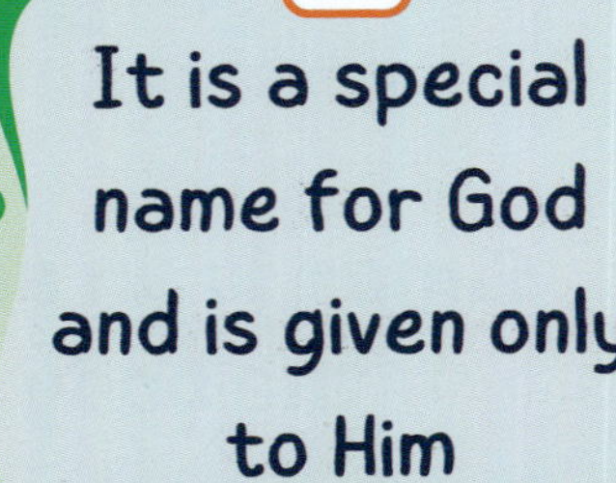

☐ It is a special name for God and is given only to Him

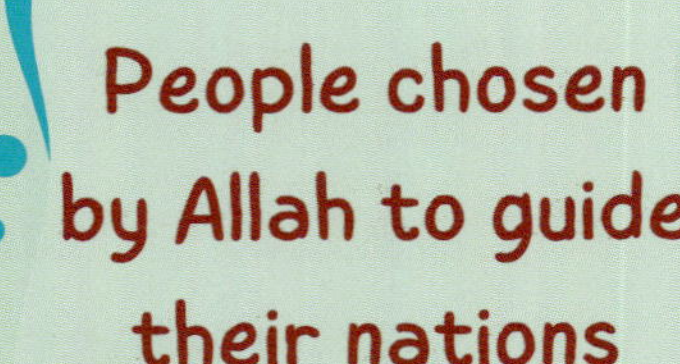

☐ People chosen by Allah to guide their nations

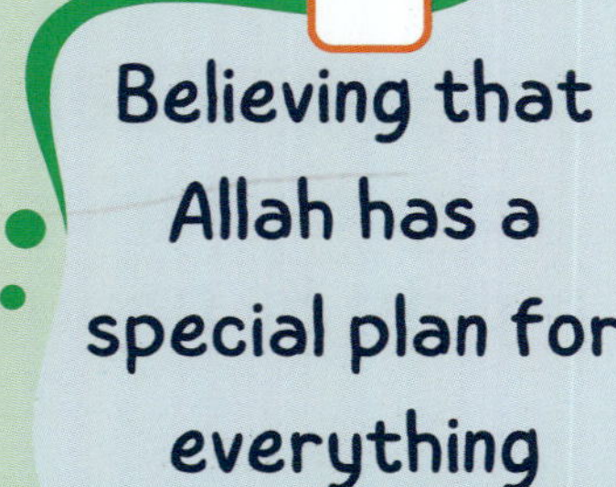

☐ Believing that Allah has a special plan for everything

☐ Placing our needs before Allah, and asking for His help

EXERCISES

True OR **False**

1. The Bible was sent to Prophet 'Adam.

2. There are seven pillars of Eiman.

3. Prophet Muhammad (PBUHF) received two books from Allah.

4. Allah has no equal or likeness.

5. We know the exact number of prophets and messengers.

6. Du'a is one of the best acts to worship Allah.

7. Allah's right upon us is to build a good life.

8. We may hate something which Allah turns into a great blessing.

Match Books With Their Prophets!

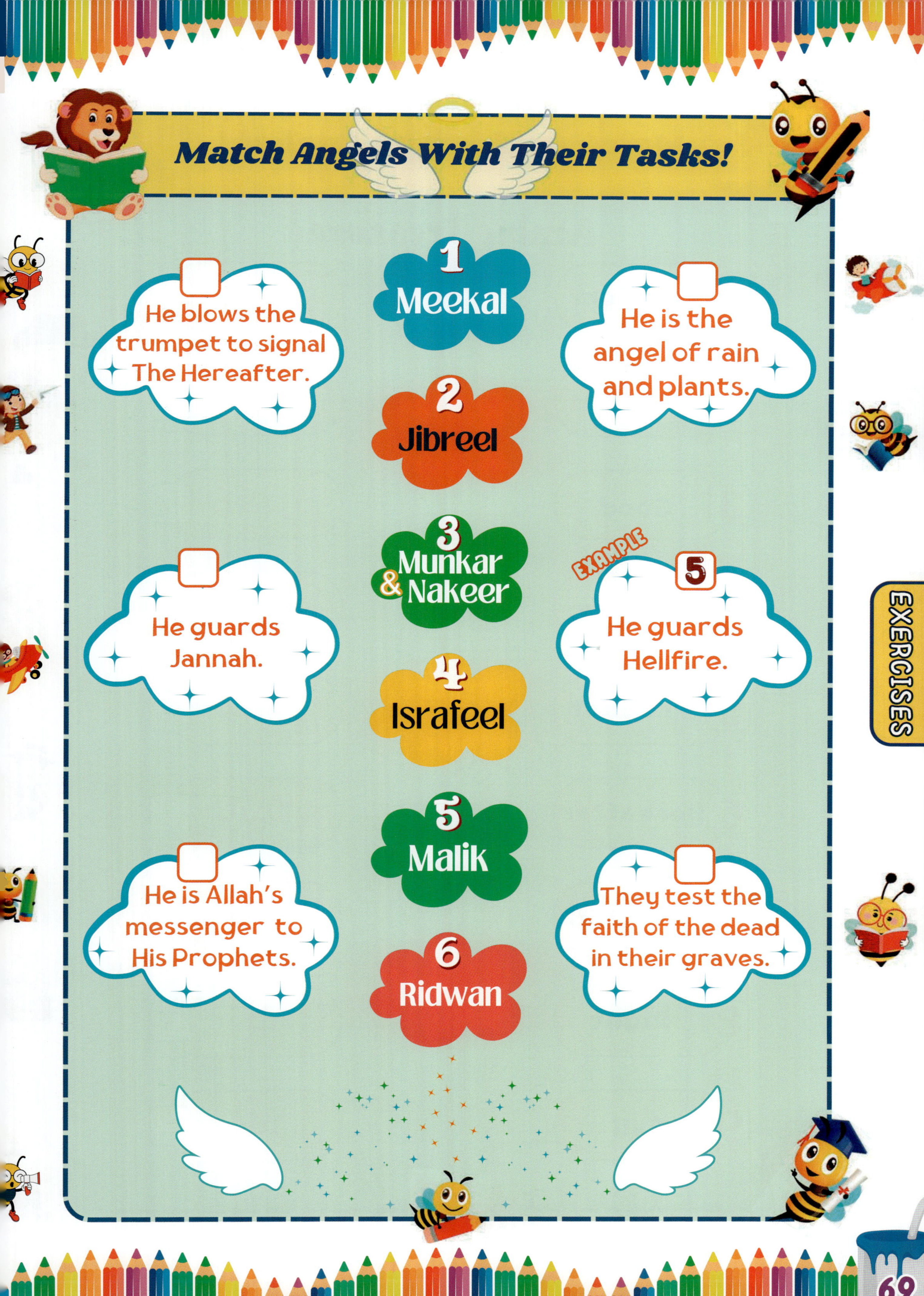

Match Angels With Their Tasks!
He blows the trumpet to signal The Hereafter.
1 Meekal
He is the angel of rain and plants.
2 Jibreel
3 Munkar & Nakeer
EXAMPLE
5
He guards Jannah.
He guards Hellfire.
4 Israfeel
5 Malik
He is Allah's messenger to His Prophets.
They test the faith of the dead in their graves.
6 Ridwan
EXERCISES
69

Match Arabic with English!

Arabic Treasure

1 Freedom	عِبَادَة ☐
2 Left	نَبِيّ ☐
3 Good	مُعْجِزَة ☐
4 Miracle	آخِرَة ☐
5 Prophet	يَمِين ☐
6 Hereafter	شِمَال ☐
7 Worship	حُرِّيَّة ☐
8 Right	خَيْر ☐
9 Evil	شَرّ ☐

Word Search Puzzle!

(Words can be found in any direction, including diagonal, and can overlap each other.)

H	I	M	E	C	C	A	Y	E	S	H	I
S	C	R	I	P	T	U	R	E	S	O	Z
B	R	O	D	E	O	S	U	N	N	A	H
C	E	U	J	I	B	R	E	E	L	R	A
O	A	Y	M	A	N	H	I	D	E	A	R
A	T	P	R	O	P	H	E	T	R	A	M
N	O	A	D	A	M	S	F	A	M	M	Q
G	R	E	A	T	T	A	B	M	H	E	U
E	N	A	M	I	E	F	A	F	T	E	R
L	O	W	N	R	I	D	W	A	N	K	A
S	O	Y	E	T	Z	I	G	O	T	A	A
Q	P	H	I	S	R	A	F	E	E	L	N

MECCA	EID	DUAA	SUNNAH
HEREAFTER	EIMAN	DESTINY	PROPHET
QURAAN	SCRIPTURES	JIBREEL	ISRAFEEL
MEEKAL	ANGELS	CREATOR	RIDWAN

EXERCISES

MANNERS

الْأَخْلَاق

MANNERS "AKHLAQ" 72

AKHLAQ EXERCISES 122

Good Manners

Lesson objectives

- To understand the importance of good manners.
- To learn manners' vocabulary.
- To practise classroom manners.

good morning PLEASE good evening thanks SORRY good night

"THE DEAREST TO MUHAMMAD" (PBUHF)

Prophet Muhammad (PBUHF)* said:

"The dearest and nearest among you to me on the Day of Judgment will be the best of you in manners".

(At-Tirmidhi)

He also told us that he was sent to perfect good character, and he used to ask Allah to protect him from bad manners.

What should we say?

When we want something

When we make a mistake

When someone helps us

THANK YOU

Allah praised Muhammad (PBUHF) in Qur'an:

"وَإِنَّكَ لَعَلَىٰ خُلُقٍ عَظِيمٍ"

"Indeed, you have great manners"

[Alqalam, 4]

*Peace Be Upon Him and his Family

School Manners

- *I must address my teachers and all staff politely.*
- *I should not interrupt an ongoing conversation unless there is an emergency.*
- *I must respect my classmates.*
- *I must raise my hand when asking or answering a question and not shout, even to get my point heard.*
- *I must have the correct equipment for my lessons.*
- *I must follow my teachers' instructions and my school's policy at all times.*
- *I must always knock on closed doors and wait for a response before entering.*

We Believe

- Teachers carry a sacred message, following the footsteps of prophets and messengers.
- Our manners reflect our religion, and we must show the correct image of our beautiful Islam.

Honouring Our Parents

Lesson objectives

- To understand parents' status in Islam.
- To learn the reward of honouring parents.
- To know how to honour your parents.

YOUR DOOR TO PARADISE

Honouring one's parents is one of the most important deeds that will lead a person to Jannah.

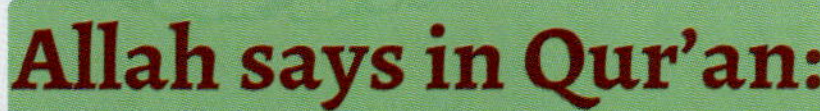

Allah says in Qur'an:

"Your Lord has ordered you to worship none except Him, and to be good to your parents" [Al-Isra', 23]

Allah also commanded us to be grateful to our parents, especially our mothers, because they carried us through hardship.

We Believe that our relationship with our parents affects directly our relationship with Allah.

Prophet Muhammad "PBUHF" said:

"Allah's pleasure results from the parents' pleasure, and Allah's displeasure results from the parents' displeasure."

(At-Tirmidhi)

A GOLDEN OPPORTUNITY

You can be wasting a golden chance If your parents, one or both of them, reach old age during your lifetime, but you don't enter Paradise.

YOUR LORD HAS COMMANDED

BE good to your parents.

Say "My Lord! Bestow on them Your Mercy as they brought me up when I was young"

Don't say to them a word of disrespect, nor shout at them!

Address them respectfully & show humility and mercy!

OUR PARENTS...OUR LIFE

Our parents' lives become all about us, and their happiness starts when we are happy. They do all that they can so we have the best in this life.

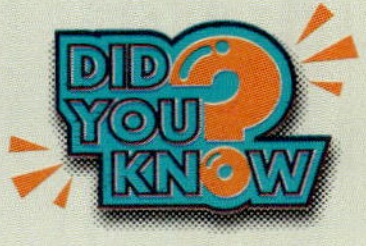

You can be good to your parents even after they pass away!

You can discuss this with your teacher/parent!

Cleanliness

Lesson objectives

- To understand the importance of cleanliness in Islam.
- My duties as a clean Muslim.

A Religion of purity & Cleanliness

Cleanliness is a way of life in Islam. Allah and His Prophet (PBUHF) encouraged us to stay clean, and we can't perform Salah without being clean (Wudu').

Muhammad's (PBUHF) companions told us that they had never smelt perfume as fragrant as the body of Prophet Muhammad (PBUHF).

Importance of Cleanliness

- **Allah's Love:** Being clean and tidy is like a secret superpower that helps us be healthy, happy, and closer to Allah!

Qur'an tells us that:

"Allah loves those who purify and clean themselves". [At-Tawbah, 108]

- **1/2 of Eiman:** The Prophet (PBUHF) also advised us to wash our hands before bed and after waking up.

The Prophet (PBUHF) said:

"cleanliness is half of our belief". (Muslim)

- **Respecting Others:** When we're clean and tidy, it shows respect for ourselves and those around us.

I'm a Muslim... I'm clean.

- **Shower Time!** Splash away the dirt with a fun shower or bath.
- **Brush, Brush, Brush!** Brushing our teeth twice a day keeps them sparkling clean and fights sugar monsters hiding in our mouths.
- **Washing Warriors!** Wash our hands before eating and after using the bathroom. We can pretend to be superheroes fighting germs with soap and water!
- **Tidy Time!** Keeping our rooms clean makes them feel like our own happy castles. Let's pick up our toys and clothes after we play!

REMEMBER!

- *Observing the cleanliness of the body, the clothes, and the surroundings is a duty upon every Muslim.*
- *We should keep our rooms, our homes, our schools, our roads, our parks, and our mosques clean.*

DID YOU KNOW? Prophet Muhammad (PBUHF) used a toothbrush 'Siwak' more than 1400 years ago, while the invention of a toothbrush is less than 250 years old!

Truthfulness

Lesson objectives

- To stimulate thinking about the importance of being truthful.
- To explore how telling the truth can be rewarding.

Ms Sarah walked into the classroom and noticed a window wouldn't open all the way. Uh oh, the handle seemed broken! "Hmm, I wonder who might have done that?" she asked the class.

Umar gulped. He'd accidentally bumped the window trying to catch a cool fly buzzing around, and SNAP! The handle went wonky. He didn't want to get in trouble, but then he remembered what his dad always said: "Being honest is the best policy, Umar. It might feel scary, but the truth always protects you in the end!"

Umar thought about having to stay in after school for extra work, but then a bigger worry popped into his head. What if Ms. Sarah didn't like him anymore? But then he thought about Allah (SWT) and how much He loves people who are honest. Even if he got in trouble, his relationship with Allah (SWT) was way more important than anything!

So, with a deep breath, Umar raised his hand. "Ms. Sarah, it was me! I broke the window handle by accident while trying to catch a fly."

Ms. Sarah's face softened instead of getting mad. "Thank you for being honest, Umar! It takes courage to admit a mistake." She even gave him a special book called "Indeed, You Have The Best Manners!" filled with stories about Prophet Muhammad (PBUHF) and how kind he always was.

Umar smiled. He learned that day that honesty might feel scary sometimes, but it's always the best choice, and it can even lead to awesome surprises!

Truthfulness leads To Jannah

Prophet Muhammad "PBUHF," said:

"Telling the truth leads to piety, and piety leads to Paradise."

(Al-Bukhari & Muslim)

He also taught us that a person will speak the truth and try hard to speak the truth until they are recorded with Allah as "Siddique". "THE SPEAKER OF TRUTH"

DID YOU KNOW?

Prophet Muhammad (PBUHF) was known as "The Truthful, The Trustworthy".

Arabic Treasure

Truthfulness	صِدْق
Truthful	صَادِق
Trustworthy	أَمِين

Generosity

Lesson objectives

- To be able to explain generosity.
- To identify examples of generosity.
- To consider ways of being generous & understand "The Joy of Giving"

Ali and Fatimah weren't your typical city kids. They lived on a farm outside Edinburgh, surrounded by fluffy sheep like Fluffy (their favourite!), silly chickens, and even a goat named Noisy! They helped their parents feed the animals every day.

Their family was super generous too! Sometimes, their mum would cook up a storm and send Ali with delicious treats for their friends down the road. At dinner time, everyone would chat about how lucky they were. "Allah has given us so much!" their dad would say, pointing around the table. "Our house, the farm, all these yummy foods. it's all thanks to Him."

"And you know what?" their mum would add with a smile, "One way to show Allah (SWT) we're grateful is by being generous to others!"

Fatimah, who had been thinking hard, suddenly had an idea. "Hey Ali," she whispered, "Remember Salman down the road? He lost his only goat, and he's been so sad ever since. Maybe... maybe we should give him Noisy?"

Now, Noisy was Ali's favourite goat. They were practically best friends! But then Ali remembered something important his dad had taught him: "Being generous doesn't mean giving away things you don't want, it's about sharing even when it's hard!"

Thinking of how sad Salman must be, Ali knew what he had to do. "You're right, Fatimah," he said with a big smile. "Allah has been so generous to us, and we have lots of goats. Sharing Noisy with Salman would be the kindest thing to do!"

With their parents' approval, Ali set off with Noisy towards Salman's house. You can imagine how happy Salman was! He was jumping out of joy. He grabbed Noisy for a big hug and thanked Ali for his generosity with a huge smile. "Jazakum Allah Khayrun," he said, which means "May Allah reward you with goodness!"

Ali might have missed Noisy a little, but knowing he'd made Salman happy made his heart sing. After all,

Allah tells us in Qur'an:

"They will never be denied the reward for any good they have done." ['Al - Imran, 115]

جزاكم الله خيرا

THE JOY OF GIVING

If you have extra toys, you can gift others and bring a smile to their faces.

Be generous with your time, talent, and kindness.

Share a meal or snacks with your friends who forgot to bring any, if it is safe to do so.*

*Some people are allergic to certain foods. Ask a responsible adult before sharing food with others.

One of the Beautiful Names of Allah is Al-Kareem The Most Generous.

Cooperation

Lesson objectives

- To understand cooperation.
- To learn examples of cooperation.
- To understand how cooperation can bring strength to our nation.

Cooperation: Working together and helping one another to the same end.

Do you think that I can make honey all by myself?

Never, Mr Human; I need 20,000 to 80,000 female worker bees to build my colony!

Allah guided us to take mountains, houses, trees, and any shelter and work together to produce honey, which is healing for you, people.

A NATION BUILT ON COOPERATION

Our beloved Prophet (PBUHF) built our Muslim nation through the teamwork of the Muslim migrants of Makkah and the Muslim supporters of Madinah.

Allah commands us in Qur'an:

"Cooperate in what is good and righteous, but don't cooperate in sin and bad deeds."

[Al-Ma'idah, 2]

Bricks aren't of much use on their own, but they can make wonders when put together.

The Prophet (PBUHF) said:

"The relationship of the believer with another believer is like (the bricks of) a building: each strengthens the other." (Al-Bukhari)

The same goes for us: working together gives us experience, strength, and various skills.

Can you give examples of achievements that are impossible without cooperation?

Here is a virtual spoonful of honey and a big clap for your hard work.

REMEMBER!

One hand couldn't have given you this big clap.

Go to pages 124-127 for exercises on Lessons 1-6.

Mercy

Lesson objectives

- To learn Allah's name (The Merciful) and discuss its meaning.
- To stimulate thinking about how to show mercy.

Mercy is one of the most significant manners a person should have. It is so important that being merciful is one of Allah's most used names.

Allah also told us that being merciful is why Prophet Muhammad (PBUHF) was very loved by his companions.

Allah tells us in Qur'an:

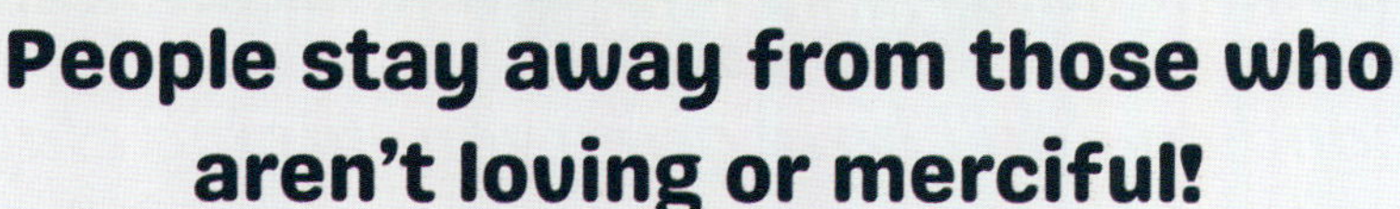

"And we have not sent you, (O Muhammad), except as a mercy to mankind." [Al-Anbeya', 107]

People stay away from those who aren't loving or merciful!

Mercy is not limited to humans; we have to be merciful towards all that is living.

The Prophet (PBUHF) said:

"Allah will have mercy on those who are merciful." (Abu Dawoud)

Prophet Muhammad (PBUHF) said:

"The believers in their mutual kindness, compassion, and sympathy are like one body.

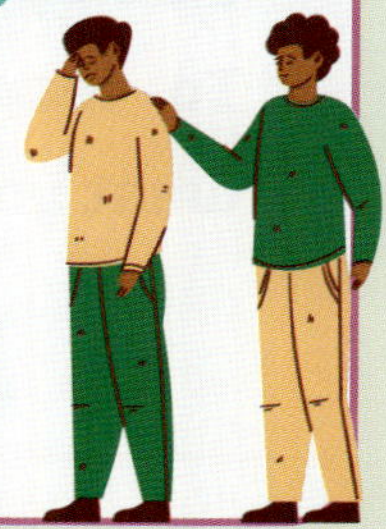

When one of the organs suffers, the whole body responds to it with wakefulness and fever."

(Al-Bukhari & Muslim)

- Mercy is a way of life. It played a key role in Prophet Muhammad's (PBUHF) success.
- Allah forgave a sinful woman and she will go to Jannah because she saved a dying thirsty dog in the desert by filling her shoe with water from a well and offering it to the dog.

REMEMBER!

We call Allah (The Most Merciful) whenever we pray or read the Qur'an.

Respecting The Elderly

Lesson objectives

- To stimulate thinking about the elderly (put yourself in their shoes).
- To learn the concept "You reap what you have sown!"

"WEAKNESS AND STRENGTH"

Allah informs us in Qur'an:

"Allah is the one who created you from weakness, then made after weakness strength, then made after strength weakness and white hair." [Ar-Room, 54]

You, I, and everyone will grow old and lose the strength we have now. Think about what you would expect from others when this happens!

Simple and yet important things: finding a seat on a bus, being able to roam with a wheelchair etc.
We have to be always there for them.

Learning about their rights and how we can observe them is a condition of being true believers, so let's explore how to give them the respect they deserve!

The Prophet (PBUHF) said:

"Not a believer, the one who doesn't acknowledge the rights of our old people." (At-Tirmidhi)

THE RESPECT THEY DESERVE

Respect and accept their **physical limitation**; they have lost most of their strength; they may not be able to walk well; They may not look as beautiful as they used to be.

Respect and accept their **mental limitation**; as people grow old, they find it harder to remember, and it takes them longer to learn new things.

HOW CAN WE SUPPORT?

Be patient when they are walking slowly in front of you.

Listen with respect, even if you are not interested in what they say.

Help!

NEVER Make Fun of Them!

SUPPORT

REMEMBER!

One day you will grow old! Think about this!

Forgiveness & Tolerance

Lesson objectives

- To define forgiveness.
- To learn Allah's name (The Forgiver)
- To understand the importance of forgiveness.

Forgiveness: It is a choice to let go of anger toward someone who hurt you, and to think, feel, or act with kindness toward that person.

WHEN PEOPLE FORGIVE,

They try to show respect to those who haven't shown respect to them.

They are kind to those who are not kind to them.

They try to be generous to those who have not been generous to them.

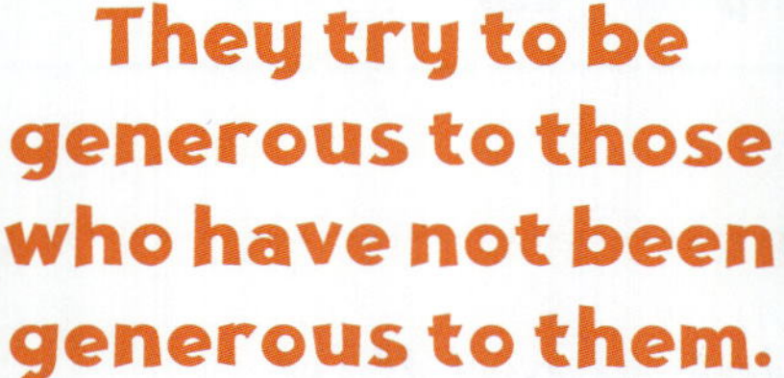

They try to be loving to their relatives even if those relatives are not loving to them.

make THE WORLD a better PLACE

Allah is The Forgiver (Al-Ghaffar), and He loves to forgive. His door is always open for us when we make mistakes.

WHY SHOULD I FORGIVE?

- When you forgive others, you are more worthy of Allah's forgiveness.

Allah tells us in Qur'an:
"Let them pardon and forgive. Do you not love to be forgiven by Allah? And Allah is All-Forgiving, Most Merciful." [An-Nour, 22]

- Forgiveness leads to healthier relationships and a better life.
- Doctors say that it is beneficial for your heart and your health in general.

REMEMBER!

Forgiveness is not being weak. It takes strength and courage to forgive.

LOVE

Lesson objectives

- To Know the value of Love in Islam.
- To recognize types of love.
- Ways to express love in Islam.

Love is a noble feeling in Islam and one of the great meanings with which a person can be happy, and it is one of the qualities that leads to Jannah.

Love of God & His Messenger

Allah Almighty told us that true believers love Him more than anything and this strong love is one of the roads to heaven.

Muhammad "PBUHF" said:

"None of you believes till I am dearer to him than his father, his child, and everyone."

(Al-Bukhari & Muslim)

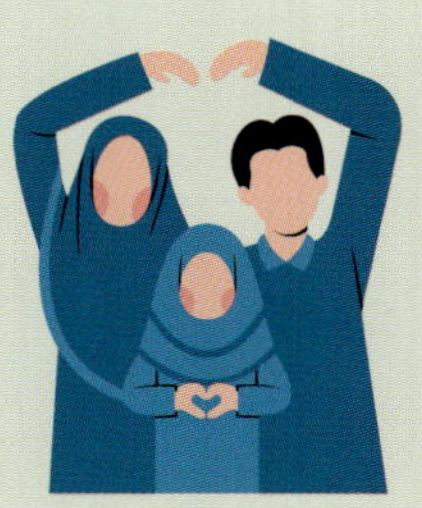

Love of Parents & Children

Parents are the source of protection, strength, and care for their children. When The Prophet (PBUHF) was asked about the best deed, he replied:

"Kindness to your parents."

(Al-Bukhari & Muslim)

I'M NOW A BELIEVER

Our beloved Prophet (PBUHF) told us that we would not enter Jannah until we believe and will not believe until we love one another. He also gave us many ways to show love for one another.

- Loving Allah and His Messenger (PBUHF) is a must for every believer.
- We can't truly love Allah, and Allah won't love us unless we follow his Prophet Muhammad (PBUHF).

Spreading Sunshine

Lesson objectives

- To learn "The power of love in Islam".
- To explore Muslim society in Madinah.
- To stimulate thinking about what a loving nation can achieve.

THE POWER OF LOVE IN ISLAM!

Imagine holding a bright, warm sunshine in your hands! It makes you feel happy and safe, right? Well, guess what? Islam teaches us that love is like sunshine. It makes everyone feel happy and warm inside!

As a Muslim, I should be loving, and I should wish for others the good life I wish for myself. Selfishness isn't Islamic.

The Prophet (PBUHF) said:

"No one of you shall become a true believer until he desires for his brother and his neighbour what he desires for himself." (Muslim)

THE WONDERFUL COMPANIONS

Al-Ansar, the Prophet's companions from Madinah, loved **Al-Mohajereen**, the Prophet's companions from Makkah, and supported them in every possible way.

Allah informs us in Qur'an:

"They love whoever immigrated to them, never having a desire in their hearts for whatever is given to the emigrants." [Al-Hashr, 9]

A ROLE MODEL TO FOLLOW

Al-Ansar split their wealth between them and Al-Mohajereen!

The companions didn't only love for each other what they loved for themselves, but they also gave others priority.

Allah tells us in Qur'an:

"They give others preference over themselves even though they may be in need." [Al-Hashr, 9]

Reaching the qualities of the Prophet's companions isn't easy, and you must train yourself to reach such a level.

DID YOU KNOW

"Prophet Muhammad (PBUHF) worked so hard to get people to become Muslims and share Jannah with him"

Smiling

Lesson objectives

- To learn smiling importance in Islam.
- To understand smiling benefits.

SMILING IS INFECTIOUS

Smiling is part of the body language that Allah has blessed us with. It is a great way to communicate and express appreciation, satisfaction, and joy.

Smiling is a universal language of kindness.

Smiling is infectious; try smiling, and you will see that all around you are smiling.

BE A SOURCE OF HAPPINESS

Smiling is a characteristic of all the prophets (PBUT). It was the key to the locked hearts of most of their nations.

Prophet Muhammad (PBUHF) was known for his smile, and his friends always loved being around him as he was their source of happiness.

Abdullah Ibn Al-Harith (RA) said:

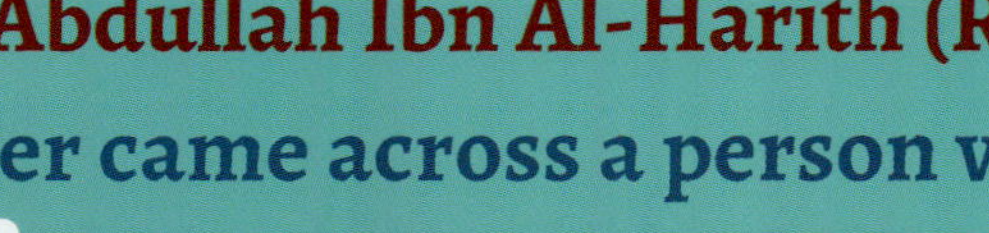

"I never came across a person who smiled as much as Prophet Muhammad."

(At-Tirmidhi)

Smiling is a prophetic sunnah, and by following it, you get rewarded.

Smiling is charity, as our master Muhammad (PBUHF) told us.

Smiling Benefits

Smiling is kindness, and spreading smiles leads to a happy life.

Smiling strengthens our immune system and leads to a healthy life.

DID YOU KNOW? The well-known smiley face we use every day was designed in 1963 by Harvey Ball, who came up with the idea of World Smile Day, which is the first Friday of October every year.

Arabic Treasure

SMILING	تَبَسُّم
LAUGHTER	ضَحِك
JOY	فَرَح

Go to pages 128-131 for exercises on Lessons 7-12.

Lying

Lesson objectives

- To understand that actions have consequences.
- To identify the moral of the story.

A young boy gets a job with a shepherd looking after his farm. Each day, he takes them up into the hills to graze. Soon, the boy felt bored: the days were long, and he felt lonely.

So, he decides to pretend there is a wolf. He shouts 'Wolf!' 'Help!' and the village farmers come running to his aid. The boy tells them the wolf has already run off, and I saved the farm.

After a couple of days, the boy was feeling bored again and decided to cry 'Wolf!' once more. When the farmers arrive and discover no wolf, they are unimpressed, and the boy can feel that they don't believe him.

The next morning, the boy is minding the sheep when a wolf appears and attacks the sheep. The boy shouts 'Wolf!' but no one comes. The farmers can hear the boy but assume he is lying.

NOBODY BELIEVES A LIAR

The farmers, who have been fooled twice, decided not to believe him. The wolf made a good meal of the boy's flock!

Do you think the farmers should have gone to his aid? **Why?/Why not?**

I'M A BELIEVER

Believers understand that all our actions are recorded, and lying leads to evil and punishment.

The Prophet (PBUHF) said:

"Avoid lying, for lying leads to wickedness, and wickedness leads to Hell." (Al-Bukhari & Muslim)

"A believer doesn't lie"

He also taught us that if a person continues to speak falsehood, and makes falsehood his object, he will be recorded as a liar before Allah.

DID YOU KNOW? There is a special home in the middle of Jannah for one who abandons lying even for the sake of fun.

Arabic Treasure

LYING	كَذِب
WOLF	ذِئْب
HELLFIRE	النَّار

Cheating

Lesson objectives

- To learn the moral of the story.
- To realise the terrible effects cheating has on individuals and society.
- To identify examples of cheating.

One night, Caliph Umar, as usual, went in disguise to check on the people. He strolled from one area to another. At last, he came to an area where poor people lived.

While passing by a small house, The Caliph heard a whispering talk within. The mother was arguing with her daughter that the milk for sale that day was very little.

She asked the daughter to mix water with milk so they could make more profit.

The daughter said, "Have you forgotten the Caliph's order?" He clarified that cheating is forbidden, and if anyone mixes water with milk, they will be punished. The mother replied, "But there is neither the Caliph nor any of his officers here to see what we do."

The daughter said, "Even if Caliph Umar does not see us, Umar's Lord still sees us; He is Ever Watching"

Imagine!

buying an apple basket to find its lower half rotten.

A developer cheats on the building material and it collapses.

A safety inspector cheats, and a faulty fire system leads to a big fire in a building.

buying a pair of shoes, but they are fake, and after 2 days only they break!

FAKE!

I'M ONE OF THE BELIEVERS.

A believer doesn't copy homework or exam answers of a friend because it is cheating.

The Prophet (PBUHF) said:

"Whoever cheats is not one of us." (Muslim)

Think of other examples of cheating!

- Cheating is forbidden in Islam in all its forms.
- If I get away with cheating in this life, Allah's punishment awaits me in 'Akhirah.
- Allah revealed Surat Al-Mutaffefeen to warn those who cheated on goods' weight in Madinah.

Hatred

Lesson objectives

- To understand hatred.
- To know the reasons for hatred.
- To find ways to overcome hatred.

IS IT THAT BAD?

You are not going to like everything and everyone. There are some things we may not like doing and some people we may not like having as friends.

Sometimes, our feelings can be even worse, and they become hatred.

You may not like certain foods!

Can I hate?

It is normal to feel hatred towards something or even someone as long as it is for the right reasons.

The Prophet (PBUHF) did not like to eat garlic and onions before going to the mosque because their smell was strong and may irritate others.

As a Muslim, I still have to behave no matter what I don't like or why. I have to be considerate and express my feelings the right way.

"BEHAVE"

Muhammad (PBUHF) never found fault with food. If he liked it, he would eat it; and if he disliked it, he would leave it. (Al-Bukhari)

Why? PEOPLE MAY HATE?

Jealousy

Injustice

Jealousy can lead to hatred. We should be happy with what we have while aiming for the best.

Avoid being unfair to others because it hardens the heart, and if it is done to you, try to forgive.

Ignorance

Rudeness

We are the enemy of what we don't know. Seek knowledge and educate yourself about others.

You captivate people's hearts with respect and love. Rudeness pushes people away.

For My Lord!

Allah is my everything. I love what He loves and hate what He hates.

Prophet Muhammad "PBUHF" said:

"The highest level of faith is when you love for Allah's sake, hate for Allah's sake." (Ahmed)

Mind Your Tongue

Lesson objectives

- To understand the power of words.
- To discuss the wrong use of the tongue.
- To learn the right use of the tongue.

Speak, so that I may see you.

Speaking shows your character and uncovers the real you to others.

People look at us Muslims, and they expect us to use good language because Allah and His Prophet (PBUHF) taught us that true believers mind their tongues.

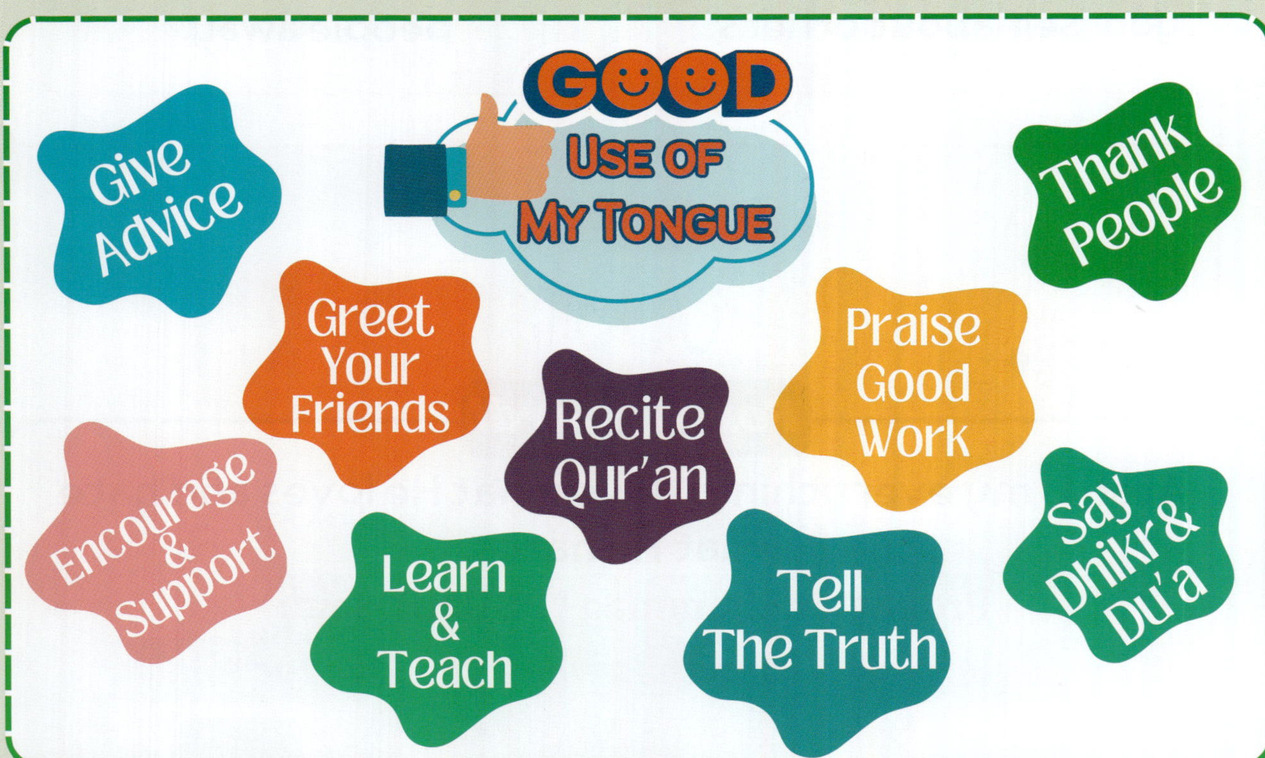

Uqbah Ibn 'Amir asked The Prophet (PBUHF):
" 'O Messenger of Allah! How can we be saved and rescued (in The Hereafter)? "

*Salvation: Rescue.

He (PBUHF) replied:
"Control your tongue."
(At-Tirmidhi)

Backbiting

Lesson objectives

- To understand the meaning of backbiting.
- To realise the impact of backbiting on our society.
- To discuss solutions to backbiting.

Ahmed, Ali, and Ibraheem met to study together. After a couple of hours, Ali had to go home. After he left, Ahmed and Ibraheem started a conversation and talked about Ali in a bad way;

HAHA!

"He is very slow." "He isn't smart." "He dresses funny." They kept laughing about him.

They were loud, and Ahmed's mum heard them. She was very annoyed and went to talk to both of them. **She explained that talking badly about someone in their absence is called backbiting, and it is a naughty thing to do even if what you say about them is true.**

naughty

She also reminded them of what Allah said in the Qur'an: And do not backbite each other. Would one of you like to eat the flesh of his brother when dead? [Al-Hujurat, 12]

"It won't happen again.
We are very sorry.
How can we fix this?"

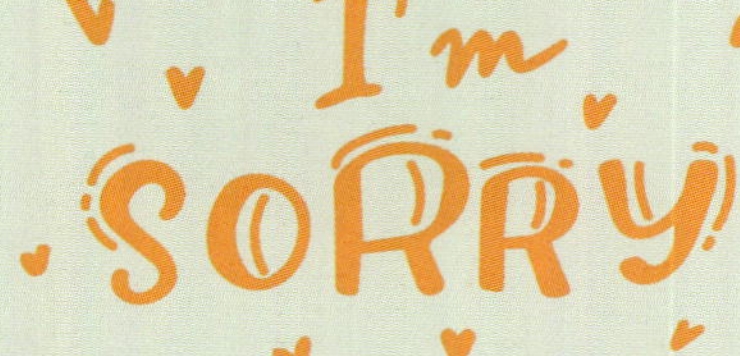

How can we fix this?

- The first step is to regret what you have done.
- Promise that you won't repeat your mistake.
- Make Du'a for the person you backbited.
- Ask Allah to forgive you and guide you.
- Give a gift to your friend so you may get closer.

Backbiting divides us and spreads hatred among us. We have to imagine the feelings of those who were backbit if they knew what was said about them.

Most importantly Allah, who knows and hears all we say. What can you tell Allah?

Ahmed and Ibraheem made a mistake, but they fixed it and listened to what Ahmed's mum told them.

They gave Ali a gift following the Prophet's advice: "Give gifts and you will love one another."

(Al-Adab Al-Mufrad)

He also asked us to give presents to one another, because a present removes bad feelings.

In the end, Ahmed, Ali and Ibraheem stayed very good friends.

Laziness

Lesson objectives

- To understand laziness.
- To learn what makes us lazy.
- To find ways to fight laziness.

Am I Lazy?

If you usually don't want to do your work or you waste your time and do your tasks very slowly, the answer is: **YES**, you are lazy.

If you usually do your work, don't waste time and do your tasks on time, the answer is: **NO**, you aren't lazy.

STAY FOCUSED!

Ask Your Lord!

"O Allah, I seek refuge in you from grief and sadness, from weakness and from laziness".

[Al-Bukhari]

"اللّهُـمَّ إنّي أَعُوذُ بِكَ
مِنَ الهَـمِّ وَ الْحَـزَنِ،
والعَجْـزِ والكَسَلِ"

Go to pages 132-135 for exercises on Lessons 13-18.

Eating Etiquette

Lesson objectives

- To understand gratefulness.
- To learn table manners.
- To memorise food Du'a.

THANK YOU, MY LORD!

As a Muslim, I understand that food and drink are a great blessing from Allah, and I should be grateful and observe Halal and Haram.

Allah tells us in Qur'an:

"O you who believe! Eat of the good things We have provided for you, and give thanks to Allah, if it is Him that you worship." (Al- Baqarah, 172)

A PROPHETIC ADVICE

Umar Ibn Abu Salamah said: I was under the care of Allah's Messenger (PBUHF), and as my hand used to roam about in the dish,

The Prophet "PBUHF" said to me:

"Boy, mention the name of Allah, and eat with your right hand and eat from what is near you." (Al-Bukhari & Muslim)

As a Muslim, I should eat and drink in moderation and not overeat. The Prophet "PBUHF," said:

"No one fills a container worse than their stomach. If he has to, then he should keep one-third for food, one-third for drink and one-third for his breathing" (At-Tirmidhi)

My Du'a... My Fortress

Before Eating

"O Allah, bless us in it and provide us with better than it"

(At-Tirmidhi)

After Eating

"Praise is to Allah Who has provided us with food, drink, and shelter, for how many are there with no food and no home?"

"الْحَمْدُ لِلَّهِ الَّذِي
أَطْعَمَنَا وَسَقَانَا، وَكَفَانَا،
وَآوَانَا، فَكَمْ مِمَّنْ لاَ
كَافِيَ لَهُ وَلاَ مُؤْوِيَ"

(Muslim)

Dressing Etiquette

Lesson objectives

- To understand modesty in dressing.
- To learn men's and women's dressing etiquette.

I Dress Modestly!

Dressing properly and modestly in Islam isn't a personal preference, but a religious requirement. There are general dressing rules that apply to everyone: boys, girls, men and women. **When we grow** and become teenagers (mature), there are special rules for males and females.

GENERAL DRESSING ETIQUETTE

When wearing, start with the right side.

Wear clean clothes

When removing, start with the left side.

Dress Modestly

Clothes must cover "*Awrah"

*Awrah: Body areas that must be covered.

When I'm older!

- My clothes must **not** be see-through or tight.
- It should not resemble men's clothing.
- The Hijab (covering) must cover the entire body except the face and the hands.

- My clothes shouldn't be see-through or tight.
- It should not resemble women's clothing.
- A man is not allowed to wear clothes made of silk, or jewellery made of gold.

Du'a of wearing clothes

"Praise be to Allah Who has given me this garment to wear and has provided it for me with no strength or power on my part".

(Abu Dawuod)

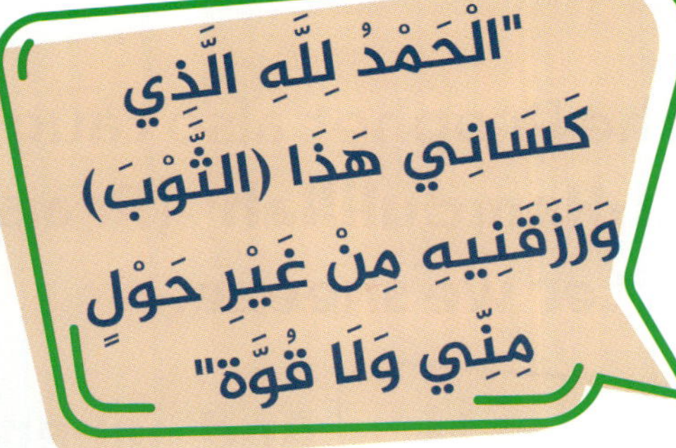

Sneezing & Yawning

Lesson objectives

- To practice the sneezing Du'a.
- To realise the difference between cultural norms and religious teachings.
- To appreciate Allah's blessings and show gratefulness.

Sneezing is an involuntary action, which means we have no control over it. One should cover their mouth with their hand or with a tissue.

"It is narrated that when The Prophet of Allah (PBUHF) sneezed, he placed his hand or a garment on his mouth and lessened the noise." (Abu Dawuod)

The Prophet also taught us to say: **Al-Hamdulillah** (Praise be to Allah), after we sneeze.

And when someone sneezes and praises Allah, we should reply, 'Yarhamuk Allah' (May Allah bestow his Mercy on you).

When the latter says 'Yarhamuk Allah' the former should say, 'Yahdikum Allah Wa Yuslih Balakum' (May Allah guide you and improve your condition)."

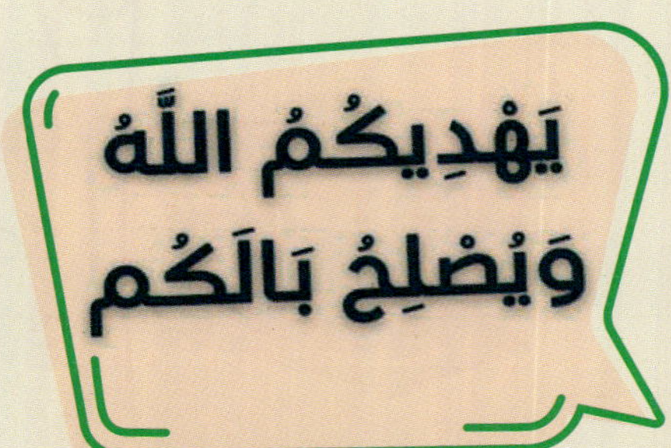

I'M ONE OF THE BELIEVERS.

If a person sneezes frequently because of a cold, it is not necessary to pray for him every time he sneezes.

This is explained by a tradition of the Prophet (PBUHF):

"Respond three times to your brother when he sneezes. If he sneezes more often, he has a cold."

(Abu Dawuod)

Yawning

Yawning is another involuntary action. We yawn because of tiredness, sleepiness, or boredom.

"When one of you yawns, he should keep his mouth shut."

(Al-Bukhari)

This is what our Prophet (PBUHF) advised us to do; we have to cover our mouths with our hands.

Activity

In pairs, practise the sneezing Du'a and take turns playing the roles, so you get to practise both roles.

DID YOU KNOW?

When a person sneezes, the heart pauses (slows down) for an instant and then resumes.

Sleep Etiquette

Lesson objectives

- To appreciate Allah's blessings.
- To learn bedtime etiquette.
- To memorise sleep & waking Du'a.

I'm a Grateful Believer!

Sleep is one of Allah's blessings upon us. Allah Almighty has made the night and day two miracles in the universe. Nighttime is important for our bodies to rest.

Allah tells us in Qur'an:

"And We have made the night and day two signs" [Al-Isra', 12]

He also told us:

"And made your sleep for rest" [An-Nab', 9]

My Lord is always with me.

Islam is a way of life for true believers. We always remember Allah and seek His guidance and protection, even when we go to bed or wake up.

Allah should be the centre of a Muslim's life.

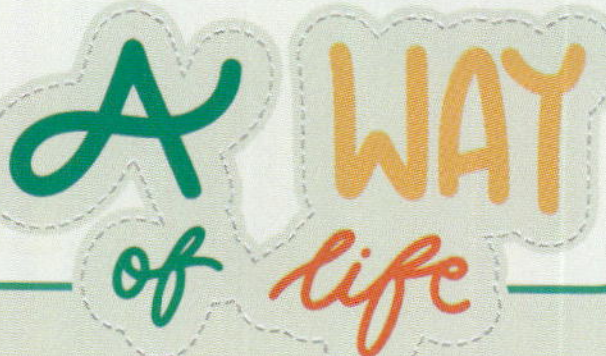

- Perform Wudu' to sleep in a state of purity.
- Dust your bed three times before sleeping.
- Lie down on your right side, put your right hand under your right cheek and recite:

"O Allah! In your Name, I live and die."

- Recite **Ayat Al-Kursi** and the last two verses of **Surat Al-Baqarah**.

My Du'a... My Fortress

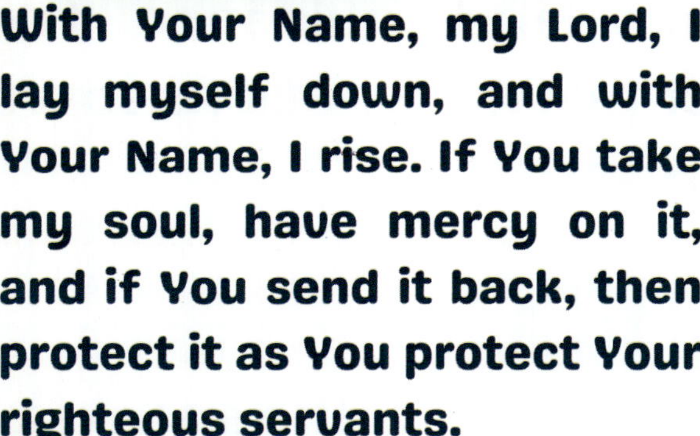

Going to Bed

With Your Name, my Lord, I lay myself down, and with Your Name, I rise. If You take my soul, have mercy on it, and if You send it back, then protect it as You protect Your righteous servants.

"بِاسْمِكَ رَبِّي وَضَعْتُ جَنْبِي وَبِكَ أَرْفَعُهُ فَإِنْ أَمْسَكْتَ نَفْسِي فَارْحَمْهَا وَإِنْ أَرْسَلْتَهَا فَاحْفَظْهَا بِمَا تَحْفَظُ بِهِ عِبَادَكَ الصَّالِحِينَ"

Waking Up

All praise is due to Allah, Who healed me in my body, and returned to me my soul, and permitted me to remember Him.

"الْحَمْدُ لِلَّهِ الَّذِي عَافَانِي فِي جَسَدِي وَرَدَّ عَلَيَّ رُوحِي وَأَذِنَ لِي بِذِكْرِهِ"

DID YOU KNOW?

Dreaming sometimes begins after about an hour and a half of deep sleep. This stage is important for the brain and mind to regain their activity.

Reciting Qur'an Etiquette

Lesson objectives

- To be able to define Qur'an.
- To understand how sacred it is.
- To learn the etiquette of reciting Qur'an.

"THE HONOURABLE QUR'AN"

- Qur'an is Allah's final message, which He sent to His last prophet, Muhammad (PBUHF).
- Qur'an was revealed and recited in Arabic, and it remains unchanged.
- It contains teachings and guidance for humans; and stories of previous nations so we can learn and take lessons.

ALLAH TALKS TO US!

Imagine that you are meeting Allah, and he speaks to you! Shouldn't you get ready for this?

Allah talks to us through Qur'an and we have to be ready to honour his message to us.

Allah tells us in Qur'an:

"Whoever honours the symbols of Allah, it is certainly out of the piety of the heart". [Al-Hajj, 32]

Let's learn together how to show respect and good manners when we recite Allah's book.

RECITATION ETIQUETTE

Think about your intention!

Perform Wudu'!

Face Qiblah If you can!

Handle Qur'an With Respect!

DON'T interrupt recitation unless necessary!

DON'T talk of fidget while reciting!

DON'T put it on the ground. Use a stand instead!

Start your recitation with the Isti`adhah and the Basmalah.

Road Manners

Lesson objectives

- To understand our moral and legal duty towards society.
- To learn road etiquette and realise its effect on life quality.

I have a Duty Towards Others

Islam teaches us that we have a responsibility towards our society and a duty towards the people we live among.

Roads and streets belong to everyone, and we must observe the law and our Islamic manners.

THE ROAD IS MY ROAD TO JANNAH

In our beautiful religion, you get rewarded for any good action. For example, Allah would forgive you and reward you with Jannah for removing any harm from the road.

The Prophet (PBUHF) said:

"While a man walks along a path, finds a thorny twig lying on the way and puts it aside, Allah would appreciate it and forgive him".

(Al-Bukhari & Muslim)

Our Prophet (PBUHF) taught us that removing stones and thorns from people's paths is Sadaqah. Guiding a person who is lost is also Sadaqah.

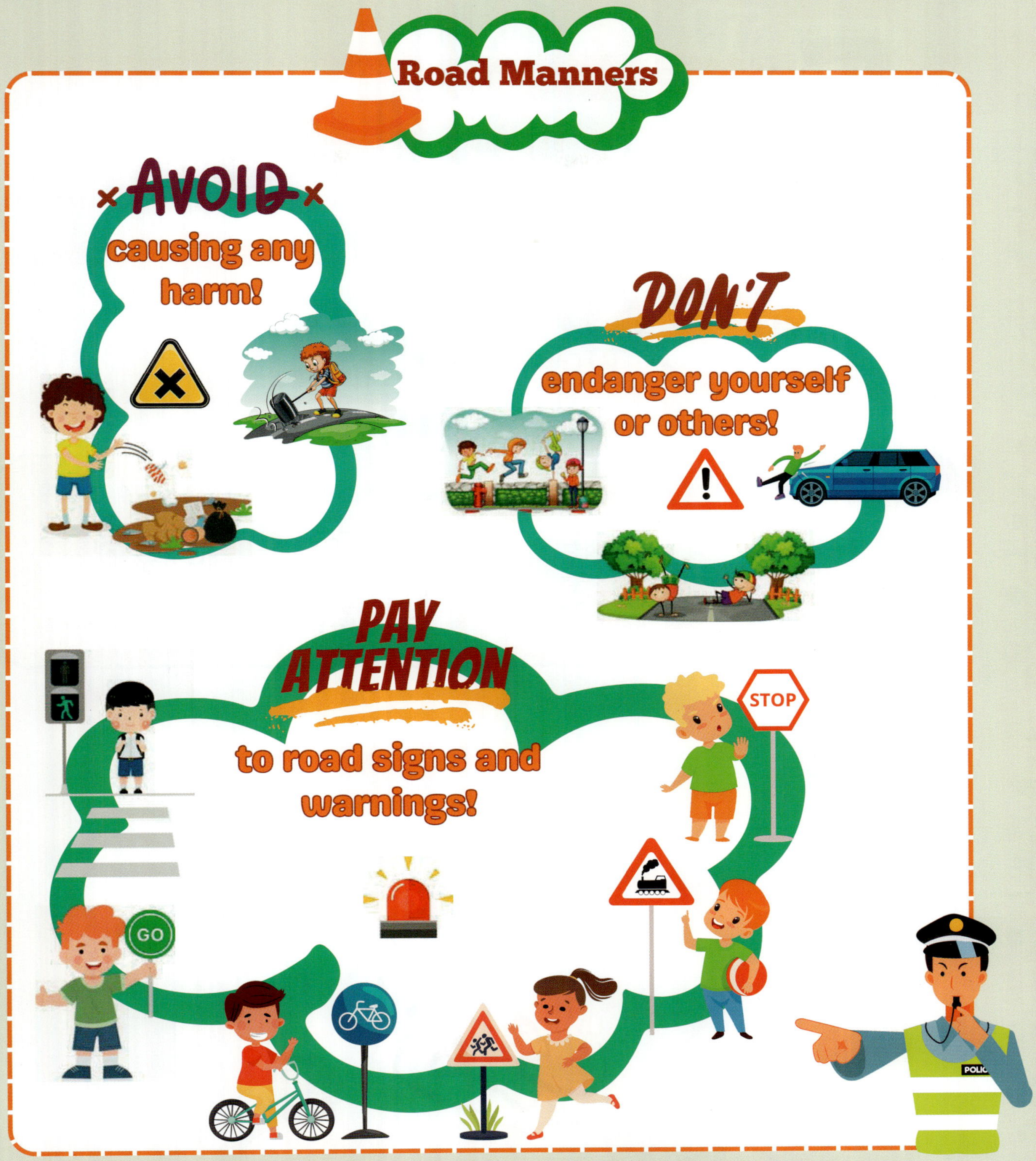
Road Manners
AVOID
causing any harm!
DON'T
endanger yourself or others!
PAY ATTENTION
to road signs and warnings!
STOP
GO
POLIC

Arabic Treasure

ROAD	طَرِيق
LIGHTS/SIGNS	إشَارَات
TRAFFIC	مُرُور

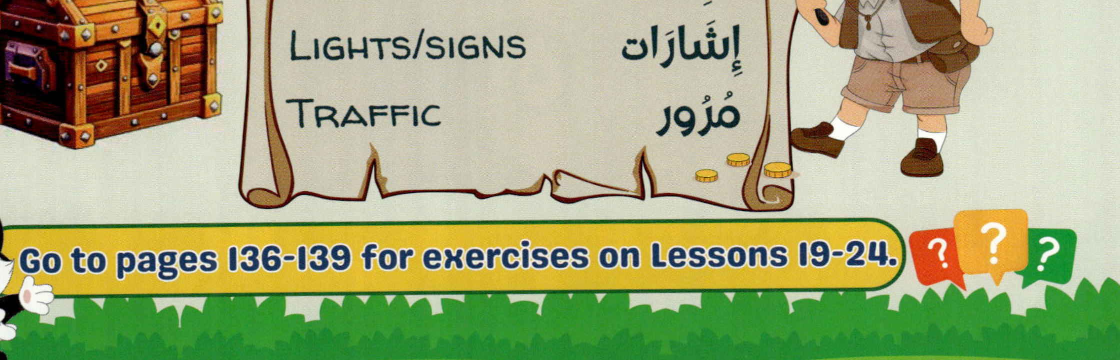

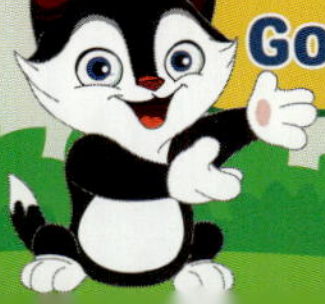

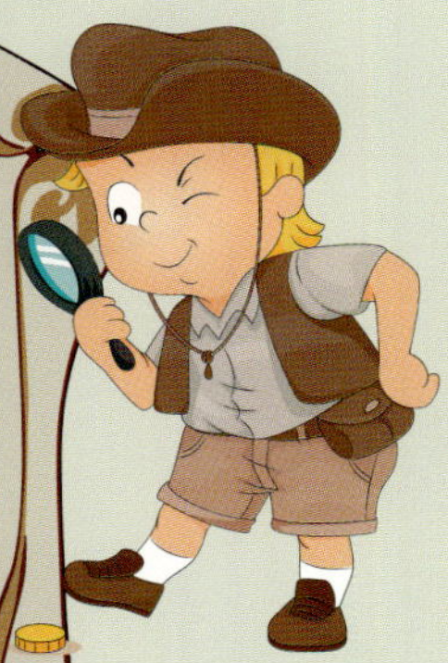

Go to pages 136-139 for exercises on Lessons 19-24.

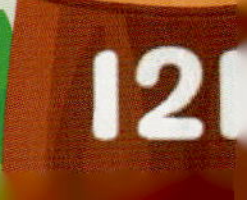

AKHLAQ

Scan QR code !

Lessons 1-6	Lessons 7-12	Lessons 13-18	Lessons 19-24

MANNERS EXERCISES

For Revision Notes and Quizzes.

For Arabic Treasure Practice

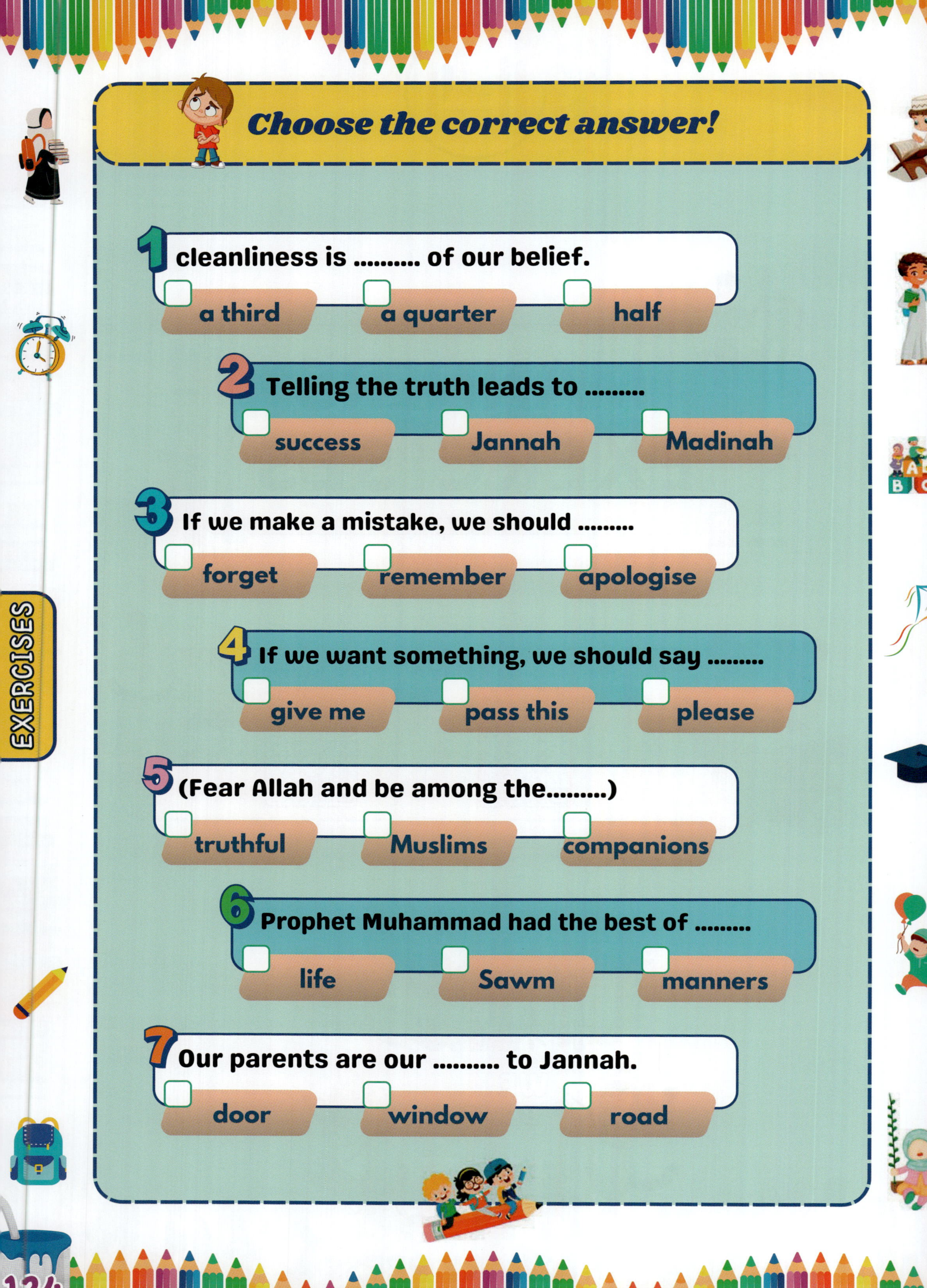

Choose the correct answer!

1. cleanliness is .... of our belief.
   - [ ] a third
   - [ ] a quarter
   - [ ] half

2. Telling the truth leads to ....
   - [ ] success
   - [ ] Jannah
   - [ ] Madinah

3. If we make a mistake, we should ....
   - [ ] forget
   - [ ] remember
   - [ ] apologise

4. If we want something, we should say ....
   - [ ] give me
   - [ ] pass this
   - [ ] please

5. (Fear Allah and be among the.........)
   - [ ] truthful
   - [ ] Muslims
   - [ ] companions

6. Prophet Muhammad had the best of ....
   - [ ] life
   - [ ] Sawm
   - [ ] manners

7. Our parents are our .... to Jannah.
   - [ ] door
   - [ ] window
   - [ ] road

EXERCISES

1. Allah commanded us to be grateful to our parents.

2. We have a responsibility to keep <u>only</u> our houses clean.

3. Your toys are yours only. You shouldn't share with others.

4. Our manners reflect our religion.

5. The Muslims of Makkah supported the migrants of Madinah.

6. Prophet Muhammad (PBUHF) was known as "The Strongest"

7. Bees are a good example of honesty.

8. Generosity is giving because you have plenty.

Match Arabic with English!
Arabic Treasure
1 Migrants
2 Cleanliness
3 Cooperation
4 Sorry
5 Manners
6 Supporters
7 Thanks
8 Truthful
9 From
أَخْلَاق
شُكْرًا
آسِف
نَظَافَة
صَادِق
مِنْ
تَعَاوُن
مُهَاجِرُون
أَنْصَار
أزهري
EXERCISES
126

Word Search Puzzle!

(Words can be found in any direction, including diagonal, and can overlap each other.)

T	S	P	O	N	M	A	N	N	E	R	S
R	S	A	X	S	A	C	R	E	D	O	R
U	E	R	S	R	D	G	O	L	Y	H	U
S	N	E	D	U	I	E	T	U	M	S	O
T	I	N	I	O	N	N	O	F	I	U	B
W	L	T	M	B	A	E	G	T	G	R	H
O	N	S	A	H	H	R	E	C	R	B	G
R	A	A	R	G	L	O	T	E	A	H	I
T	E	R	Y	I	O	U	H	P	N	T	E
H	L	E	P	E	V	S	E	S	T	O	N
Y	C	H	O	N	E	Y	R	E	S	O	I
S	U	P	P	O	R	T	E	R	S	T	H

SUPPORTERS	MIGRANTS	TRUSTWORTHY	MANNERS
TOOTHBRUSH	LOVE	CLEANLINESS	NEIGHBOURS
HONEY	MADINAH	PYRAMIDS	TOGETHER
GENEROUS	RESPECTFUL	PARENTS	SACRED

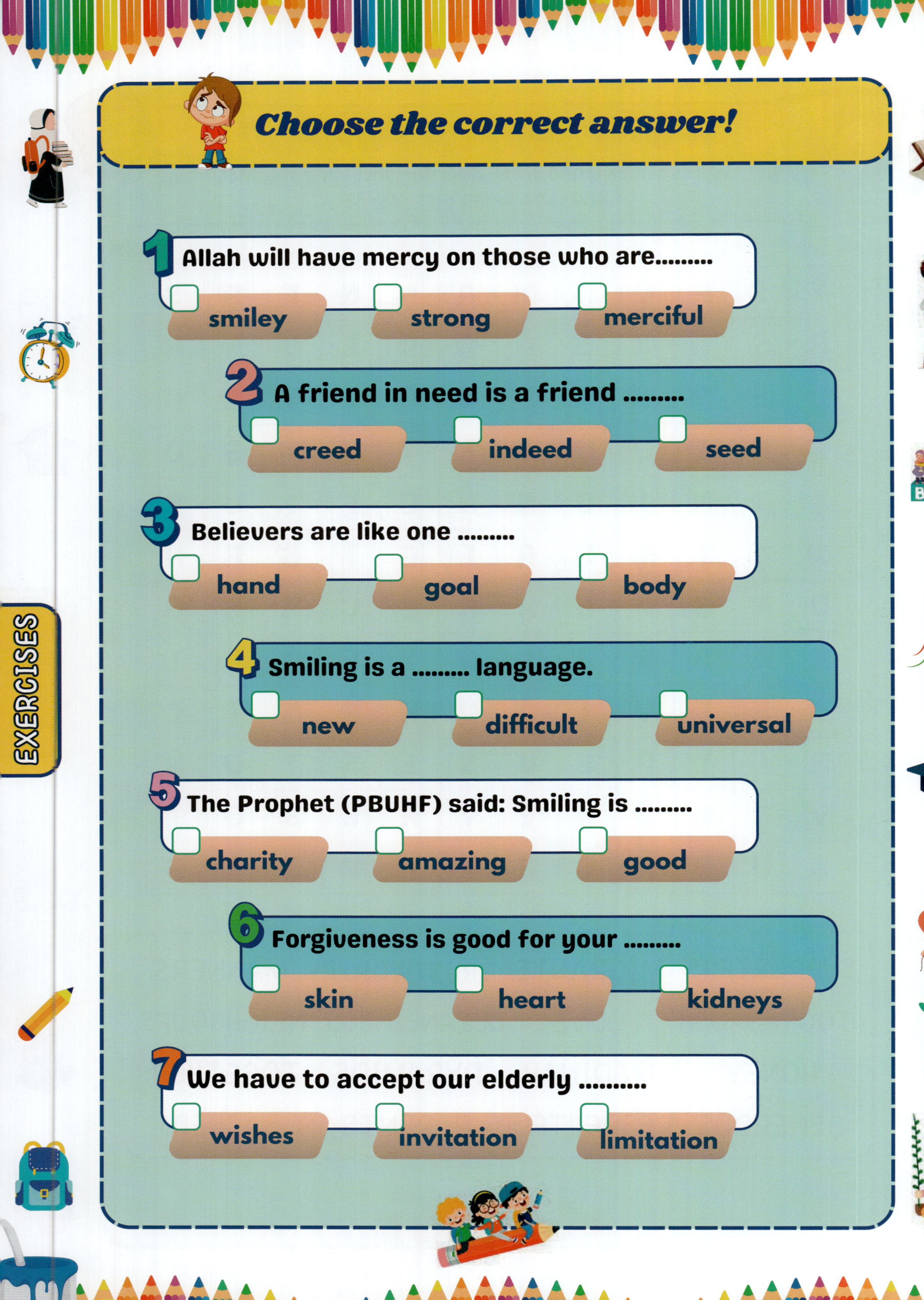

Choose the correct answer!

1. Allah will have mercy on those who are.........
   - [ ] smiley
   - [ ] strong
   - [ ] merciful
2. A friend in need is a friend ....
   - [ ] creed
   - [ ] indeed
   - [ ] seed
3. Believers are like one ....
   - [ ] hand
   - [ ] goal
   - [ ] body
4. Smiling is a .... language.
   - [ ] new
   - [ ] difficult
   - [ ] universal
5. The Prophet (PBUHF) said: Smiling is ....
   - [ ] charity
   - [ ] amazing
   - [ ] good
6. Forgiveness is good for your ....
   - [ ] skin
   - [ ] heart
   - [ ] kidneys
7. We have to accept our elderly ....
   - [ ] wishes
   - [ ] invitation
   - [ ] limitation

EXERCISES

1. We have to be merciful towards all that is living.

2. Allah forgave a sinful woman who saved a cat.

3. Al-Ansar gave half their wealth to Al-Mohajreen.

4. The World Smile Day is on the 31st of March.

5. We call Allah (The Most Merciful) whenever we read Qur'an

6. Loving Allah and His Messenger is an option for every believer.

7. When we forgive, we give away our rights.

8. Treat others the way you would like to be treated.

Match Arabic with English!

Arabic Treasure

1 Smiling	رَحْمَة
2 Mercy	رَحِيم
3 Laughter	كَلْب
4 Merciful	تبَسُّم
5 Joy	ضَحِك
6 Dog	فَرَح
7 Forgiver	كَرِيم
8 Trust	غَفَّار
9 Generous	أَمَانَة

أزهري

Word Search Puzzle!

(Words can be found in any direction, including diagonal, and can overlap each other.)

Y	B	A	R	A	F	F	A	H	G	L	A
A	L	L	A	H	M	E	N	T	A	L	L
L	A	H	E	A	L	T	H	E	A	I	M
U	I	O	N	E	M	E	V	N	R	M	O
F	C	W	A	V	L	E	S	I	R	I	H
R	I	K	M	O	I	A	Y	M	A	T	A
E	F	O	I	L	R	V	E	S	H	A	J
D	E	O	E	R	A	M	L	I	E	T	E
N	N	B	M	T	R	A	E	H	E	I	R
O	E	V	I	G	R	O	F	R	M	O	O
W	B	E	L	I	E	V	E	Y	C	N	U
S	M	I	L	E	L	D	E	R	L	Y	N

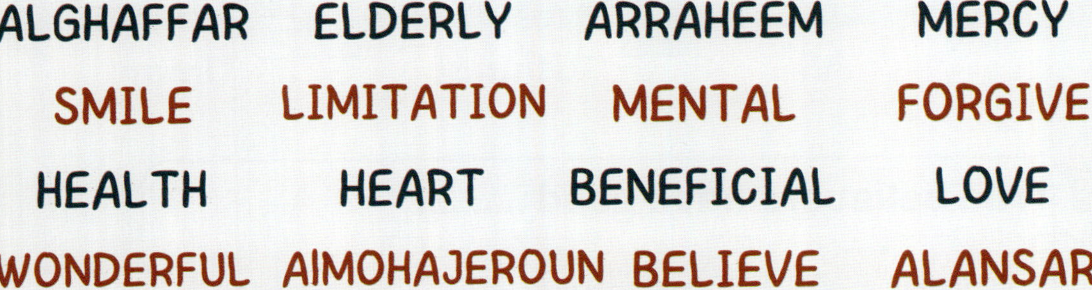

ALGHAFFAR ELDERLY ARRAHEEM MERCY
SMILE LIMITATION MENTAL FORGIVE
HEALTH HEART BENEFICIAL LOVE
WONDERFUL AIMOHAJEROUN BELIEVE ALANSAR

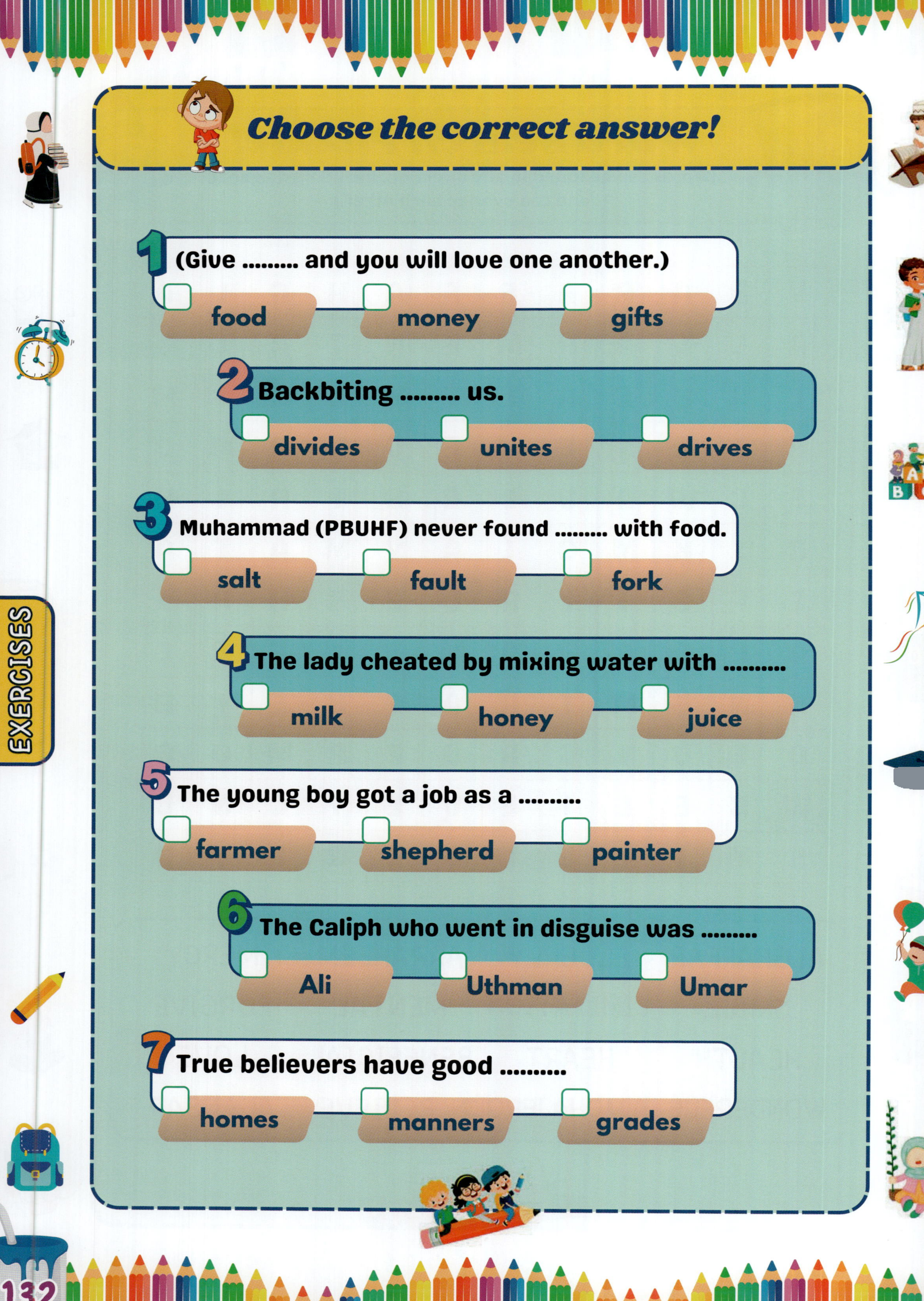

Choose the correct answer!

1. (Give .... and you will love one another.)
   - [ ] food
   - [ ] money
   - [ ] gifts

2. Backbiting .... us.
   - [ ] divides
   - [ ] unites
   - [ ] drives

3. Muhammad (PBUHF) never found .... with food.
   - [ ] salt
   - [ ] fault
   - [ ] fork

4. The lady cheated by mixing water with ....
   - [ ] milk
   - [ ] honey
   - [ ] juice

5. The young boy got a job as a ....
   - [ ] farmer
   - [ ] shepherd
   - [ ] painter

6. The Caliph who went in disguise was ....
   - [ ] Ali
   - [ ] Uthman
   - [ ] Umar

7. True believers have good ....
   - [ ] homes
   - [ ] manners
   - [ ] grades

1. Nobody believes a liar.

2. There is a nice home in Jannah for one who abandons lying.

3. Allah revealed Surat Al-Mutaffefeen to warn those who lie.

4. The Prophet (PBUHF) did not like to eat garlic before going to the mosque.

5. It is normal to feel hatred towards something or even someone.

6. Controlling your tongue saves you in The Hereafter

7. The highest level of faith is to be kind and to pray a lot.

8. Backbiting divides us and spreads hatred among us.

Match Arabic with English!

Arabic Treasure

1 silence	كَـذِب
2 Lazy	ذِئْـب
3 Gossip	الـنَّار
4 Lying	أَمْسِك
5 Hellfire	نَمِيمَة
6 Wolf	لِسَان
7 Control	غَـيْـبَة
8 Tongue	كَـسْـلَان
9 Backbiting	صَـمْـت

Word Search Puzzle!

(Words can be found in any direction, including diagonal, and can overlap each other.)

I	C	A	N	U	C	A	N	L	A	Z	Y
S	U	P	P	O	R	T	M	E	Y	M	K
L	B	A	R	Y	U	T	O	C	S	I	L
A	A	Z	G	E	D	O	C	I	U	S	C
M	C	B	N	V	E	N	K	T	O	T	O
A	K	O	I	E	N	G	I	S	L	A	N
H	B	A	R	I	E	U	N	U	A	K	T
M	I	S	A	L	S	E	G	J	E	E	R
O	T	T	E	E	S	O	O	N	J	F	O
U	I	I	W	B	V	G	N	I	Y	L	L
D	N	N	S	E	O	P	I	S	S	O	G
Y	G	G	S	I	L	E	N	C	E	W	R

WOLF	SILENCE	GOSSIP	LYING
LAZY	CONTROL	TONGUE	BACKBITING
MISTAKE	MOCKING	SWEARING	BOASTING
SUPPORT	INJUSTICE	RUDENESS	JEALOUSY

EXERCISES

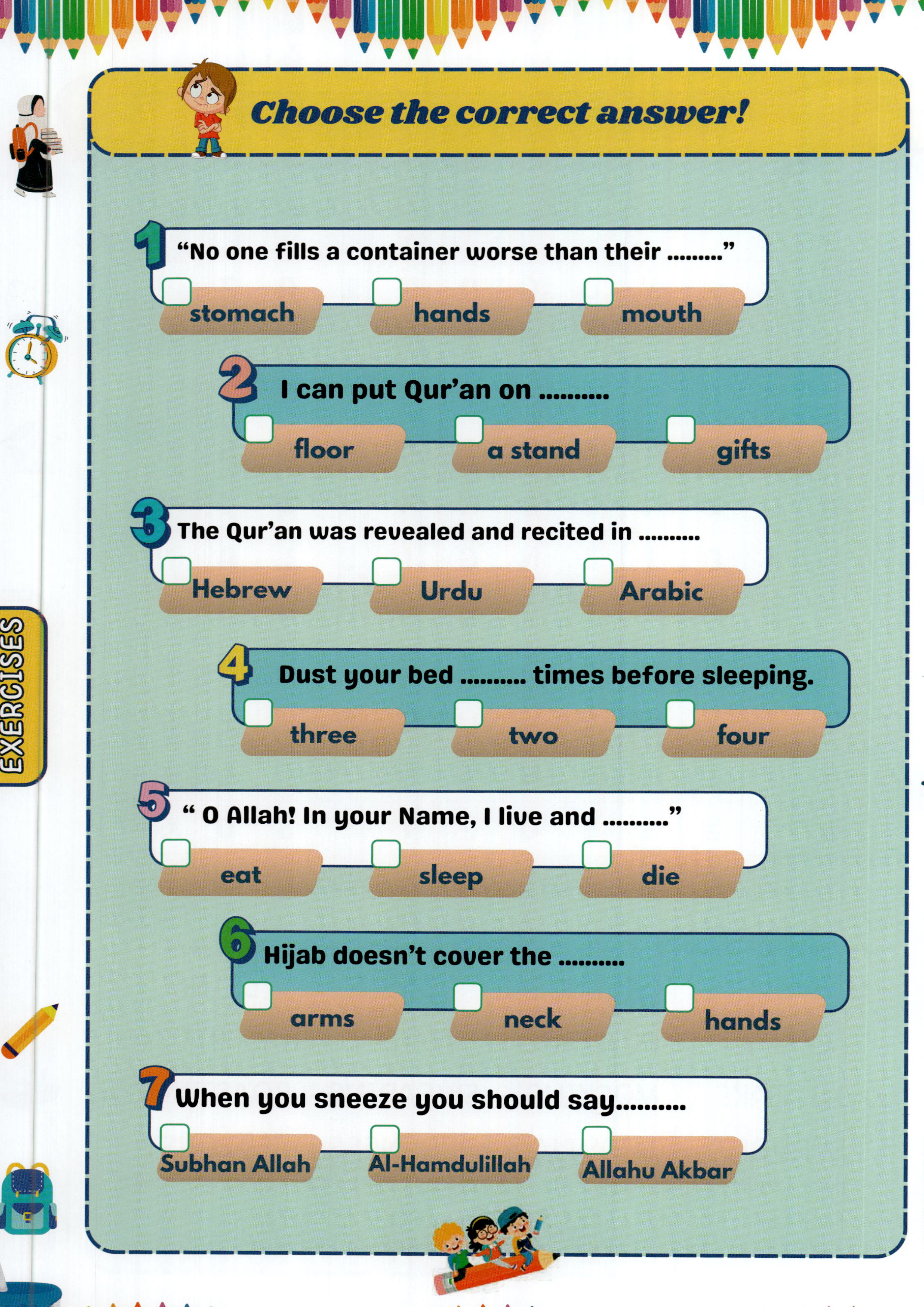

Choose the correct answer!

1 "No one fills a container worse than their ...."

- [ ] stomach
- [ ] hands
- [ ] mouth

2 I can put Qur'an on ....

- [ ] floor
- [ ] a stand
- [ ] gifts

3 The Qur'an was revealed and recited in ....

- [ ] Hebrew
- [ ] Urdu
- [ ] Arabic

4 Dust your bed .... times before sleeping.

- [ ] three
- [ ] two
- [ ] four

5 " O Allah! In your Name, I live and ...."

- [ ] eat
- [ ] sleep
- [ ] die

6 Hijab doesn't cover the ....

- [ ] arms
- [ ] neck
- [ ] hands

7 When you sneeze you should say..........

- [ ] Subhan Allah
- [ ] Al-Hamdulillah
- [ ] Allahu Akbar

1. Removing harm from roads is Sadaqah.

2. When taking off your shoes, start with the right one.

3. In Islam, you get rewarded for any good action.

4. You should keep two-thirds of your stomach for food.

5. Dressing properly in Islam is a personal preference.

6. A man is not allowed to wear clothes made of silk.

7. When sleeping, lie down on your left side.

8. We have a responsibility towards our society.

Match Arabic with English!

Arabic Treasure

1 Recitation	نِعْمَة	☐
2 Clothes	طَعَام	☐
3 Shirt	شَرَاب	☐
4 Traffic	مَلَابِس	☐
5 A blessing	قَمِيص	☐
6 Signs	تِلَاوَة	☐
7 Food	طَرِيق	☐
8 Drink	إِشَارَات	☐
9 Road	مُرُور	☐

Word Search Puzzle!

(Words can be found in any direction, including diagonal, and can overlap each other.)

D	O	S	N	E	E	Z	I	N	G	C	O
A	T	M	A	Z	H	A	R	Y	N	L	Q
O	R	G	A	N	I	S	A	T	I	O	N
R	A	N	E	O	J	A	B	L	S	T	O
E	F	I	A	U	A	L	A	O	S	H	I
S	F	N	T	R	B	L	O	V	E	E	T
E	I	A	I	D	A	A	M	E	L	S	A
M	C	E	N	H	L	H	Y	L	B	C	T
B	R	M	G	I	H	O	D	A	O	O	I
L	Y	A	W	N	I	N	G	O	S	V	C
E	O	D	R	E	S	S	I	N	G	E	E
J	E	W	E	L	L	E	R	Y	O	R	R

RECITATION	ROAD	MEANING	TRAFFIC
BLESSING	CLOTHES	COVER	HIJAB
JEWELLERY	RESEMBLE	GOLD	SNEEZING
YAWNING	DRESSING	HALAL	EATING

EXERCISES

6TH

Prophets' Stories

قَصَصُ الأَنْبِيَاء

WWW.AZHARY.ORG

أَزْهَرِيّ

ALMOST
THERE!

Why do we need to learn their stories?

We Believe in all prophets and messengers Allah sent, and we must learn their stories to understand what we believe about them.

Allah told us in Qur'an that:

"In their stories, there is truly a lesson for people of sound minds." (Yousuf, 111)

Allah also told us that he narrated to Prophet Muhammad (PBUHF), the best stories in Qur'an. Allah told him to tell these stories to us, perhaps we will reflect and learn from them.

The Best Of Role Models

Allah chose His messengers as they were the best in their nations and each one of them is a role model for us to follow.

We should show the highest respect when talking about them, send Salam and prayers upon them and we should love all of them equally.

Prophet Muhammad "PBUHF," said:

"Do not prefer some prophets to others"

(Al-Bukhari)

- **Prophet Muhammad is the best of Allah's creation, and we respect all prophets.**
- **Allah sent many messengers and has told us in Qur'an the stories of some of them, while others He has not.**

Nouh (PBUH)

2

Many years after **Prophet 'Adam** (PBUH), people started to pray to idols instead of Allah.

Prophet Nouh "Noah" (PBUH) tried to warn them that if they did not stop praying to idols, Allah would punish them.

But the people did not listen to him and would put their fingers in their ears so they could not hear him speak.

We Believe that He kept advising them day and night for 950 years, but only a few listened.

Allah told us in Qur'an that Prophet Nouh said:

"And whenever I invite them to be forgiven by You, they press their fingers into their ears, cover themselves with their clothes, persist ⌜in denial⌝, and act very arrogantly." (Nouh, 7)

Prophet Nouh talked to his people in public and privately. He explained to them that the five idols they worship are just statues named after good people who died; the statues were to keep their memory alive.

He also warned them of Allah's punishment if they kept refusing His message.

Allah told us in Qur'an that they said to Nouh (PBUH): "O Nouh! You have argued with us far too much, so bring upon us what you threaten us with, if what you say is true." (Houd, 32)

Prophet Nouh replied that It is Allah Who can bring it upon them if He wills, and then they will have no escape.

Allah revealed to Nouh that no more people will believe except those who already have. So do not be distressed by what they have been doing, and build the **Ark**. So he began to build the Ark, and whenever some of the chiefs of his people passed by, they mocked him.

Imagine building a ship in the middle of the desert! and by yourself!

Prophet Nouh always had Allah with him; whoever puts his trust in Allah, He shall be enough for them.

After finishing The Ark, he took into it a pair from every species, along with the believers and family except those who rejected the message.

And he said,

"Board it! In the Name of Allah, it will sail and In the Name of Allah, it will anchor." (Houd, 41)

Soon after, heavy rains poured down from the angry skies, and water began to rise through every crack on earth. The oceans filled the land; The Ark floated carrying the believers.

Those who used to laugh at Prophet Nouh are screaming now as they drown.

The Ark sailed with them through waves like mountains. Nouh (PBUH) called out to his son, who stood apart,

"O, my dear son! Come aboard with us and do not be with the disbelievers."

His son replied, "I will take refuge on a mountain, which will protect me from the water."

Nouh cried, "Today no one is protected from Allah's decree except those to whom He shows mercy!"

And the waves came between them, and his son was among the drowned.

The Ark kept sailing with the mercy of Allah, and the believers were thankful to their Lord and their Prophet who guided them and saved them from the punishment.

Allah commanded the earth to swallow up its water and the sky to withhold its rain. Prophet Nouh & those who followed him, survived, but the rest drowned.

The skies immediately cleared, and the sun shone brightly on the land. Meanwhile, Nouh's ark peacefully landed on Mount Judi.

Allah instructed His Prophet:

"O, Nouh! Come down (from the ship) with peace from Us and blessings on you and the people who are with you."

(Houd, 48)

Prophet Nouh, along with the believers, got off the ark. They released the animals, birds and insects across the land.

They also placed their foreheads on the ground, praising Allah, their Lord, and thanking Him greatly for His mercy and blessings.

The story of Prophet Nouh and his nation was used by most of the prophets who came after him as a reminder to other nations and as an example to learn from.

All messengers of Allah are brave and patient. Allah chose five to be the most special; Prophet Nouh is one of the chosen five.

Moral of The Story

- We should be patient and learn from Prophet Nouh not to give up.
- We should listen to Allah's commands and trust him; Prophet Nouh built an Ark in the desert!
- Our parents love us and want the best for us; we should obey and respect them.
- Laughing at others and being too proud of yourself is not what Muslims do. Look at what happened to those who laughed at Nouh (PBUH)!

Scan QR code! For Revision Notes and Quizzes.

AZHARY PRESS

Rearrange The Story Events!

After finishing The Ark, he took into it a pair from every species.

Prophet Nouh invited his people to worship Allah, but they didn't listen.

Allah made the earth swallow up its water. Nouh's Ark landed on Mount Judi.

Heavy rains poured, and the oceans filled the land. His son didn't survive.

The Ark sailed with them through waves like mountains, and the believers survived.

Allah told Nouh (PBUH) to build an ark. His people laughed at him.

EXERCISES

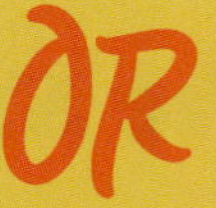

1. Prophet Nouh's son listened and survived at the end.

2. Nouh (PBUH) kept advising his people for 950 years.

3. His nation worshipped 5 statues named after people who died.

4. Prophet Nouh built an Ark near the river as he loved sailing.

5. He took one animal from every species on his Ark.

6. Prophet Nouh's ark peacefully landed on Mount Sinai.

7. All messengers of Allah are brave and patient.

8. Allah chose five Prophets to be the most special; Nouh (PBUH) is one of them.

EXERCISES

Word Search Puzzle!

(Words can be found in any direction, including diagonal, and can overlap each other.)

I	N	S	U	R	E	S	E	G	O	O	D
P	A	I	R	H	O	O	V	E	R	F	I
S	M	Q	U	E	A	N	I	M	A	L	M
U	M	O	J	O	V	R	F	C	L	O	O
R	N	E	U	V	U	E	K	H	A	O	C
V	O	I	D	N	A	S	I	A	I	D	K
I	W	K	I	E	T	B	O	L	C	I	E
V	O	W	P	O	S	A	N	A	E	A	D
E	M	E	R	C	Y	E	I	H	P	B	Q
D	O	T	A	M	M	A	R	N	S	L	W
I	D	A	E	R	E	A	L	T	O	O	E
R	H	A	R	A	S	O	N	I	H	K	D

NOUH	ARK	MOUNTAIN	JUDI
PAIR	ANIMAL	BELIEVERS	SON
DESERT	FLOOD	SURVIVED	MERCY
SPECIAL	FIVE	MOCKED	EARS

Younus (PBUH)

Younus Ibn Matta was a messenger of Allah. He was born and grew up among the people of Nineveh in the northern area of Iraq with over a hundred thousand people.

The city of Nineveh had long forgotten the message of Allah and became a city filled with idol worshipping and sin. Allah sent Prophet Younus to guide them to Allah.

But the people of Nineveh rejected Younus, just as many nations rejected the prophets and messengers before him.

He continued to call them to worship Allah, reminding them of Allah's anger over the people of Nouh and other nations.

Prophet Younus wanted to help his people. He did not give up on them; despite their harsh words, he continued to warn them of Allah's punishment.

"Let it happen", the men laughed and informed Younus that they were not the least afraid of his threats.

Prophet Younus was sad; he gave up on his people. Without the permission of Allah, he decided to leave the city of Nineveh in hopes of finding a community far away that would accept him and Allah's message.

He boarded a small passenger ship to travel as far away from his people as possible.

The ship travelled during the day through the calm waters. As the night came, a storm rocked the boat. It was really dangerous.

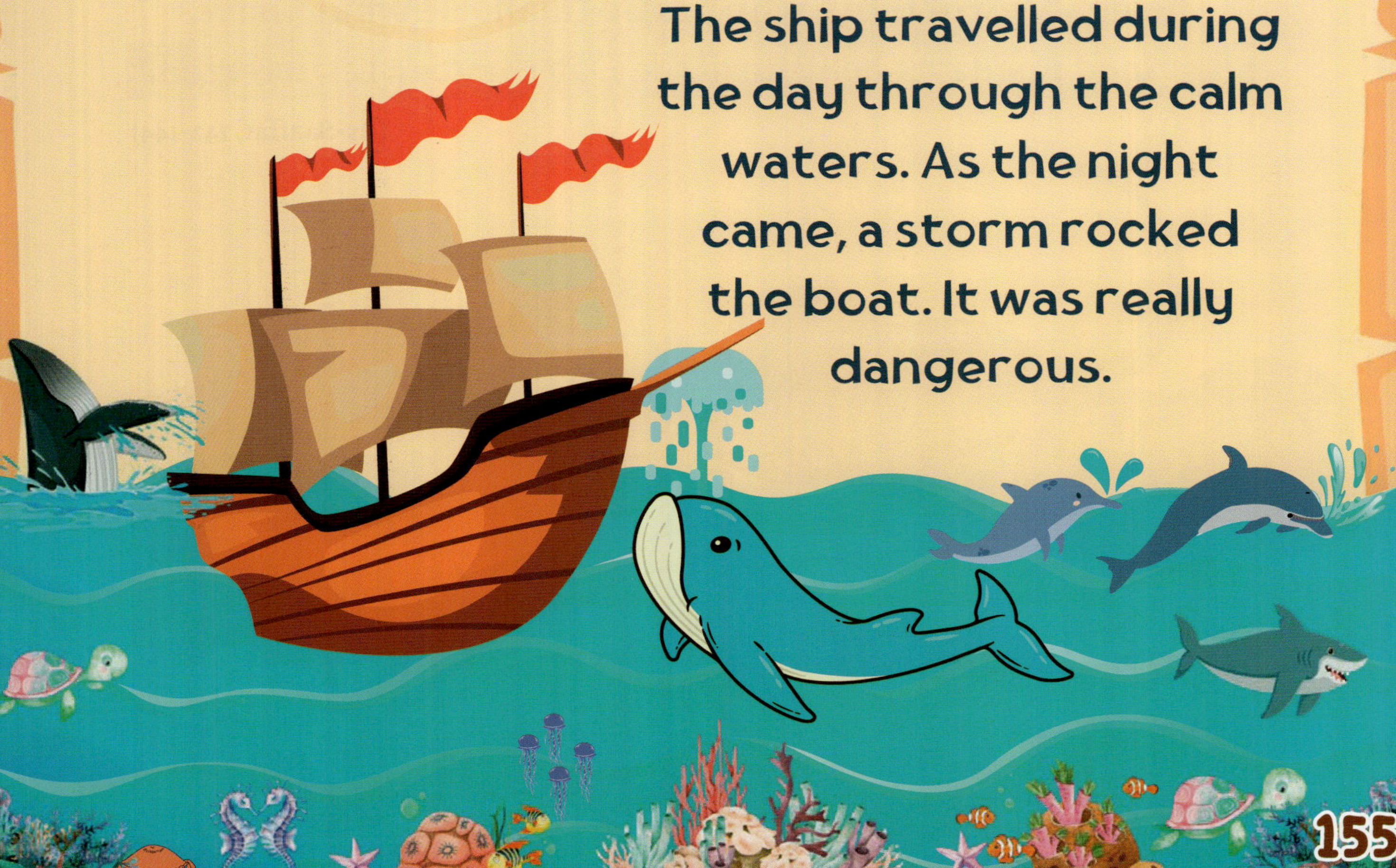

The sailors threw out all of the extra things; but, the ship was still heavy and continued to sink.

The passengers began to fear for their lives as the sea water gradually flooded the deck, slowly sinking the ship.

They needed to choose someone to be thrown into the sea. The random choice was Prophet Younus. People knew he was a man of Allah, so they chose again and again. The result was always Prophet Younus. He jumped into the dark, angry waves in the middle of the ocean.

"Then the fish swallowed him, while he was to blame. And had he not been of those who praise Allah, He would have remained inside its belly until the Day they are resurrected."

(As-Saaffat, 142-144)

As Allah commanded, the largest whale in the ocean swallowed Younus (PBUH) just as he hit the water. He awoke to find himself in darkness.

Prophet Younus, knowing that no one could save him but Allah, started praying.

"And he called out within the darknesses: There is no lord except You. Indeed, I have been one of the wrongdoers."

(Al-Anbeya', 87)

Allah the Most Merciful answered his messenger's prayer and commanded the whale to spit him out at the shore.

When Younus (PBUH) recovered, he travelled back to Nineveh to complete his mission. Upon arriving, he found out that everyone had already believed in Allah!

After Prophet Younus had left, the calm sky over Nineveh turned red, and it seemed that Allah's punishment had started.

Everyone gathered on top of the hills with their hearts filled with fear. Now, They remembered Prophet Younus's warning of Allah's punishment.

They were scared that they would face what the people of Nouh, 'Ad and Thamoud had faced.

Falling on their knees, they raised their hands and begged Allah for forgiveness and mercy. They truly regretted the way they treated Prophet Younus and prayed for his return.

Allah forgave them and lifted His punishment. The sky was back to normal, and every single person became a true believer.

All this happened while Younus (PBUH) was away, and that's why he was surprised upon arrival.

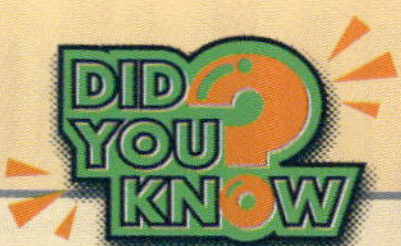

Younus was the only Prophet whose entire nation accepted his message.

Allah stated in the Holy Qur'an regarding the people of Younus (PBUH):

"Was there any nation that believed after seeing the punishment, and its faith saved it from the punishment?" (Younus, 89)

Allah also told us that the answer is none except the people of Younus; when they believed, Allah lifted the punishment.

Moral of The Story

- We should learn from others' mistakes and be wise not to repeat what they did.
- Allah gives us many chances before he punishes us, and we should be grateful to him.
- If you do something wrong, seek forgiveness from Allah; Allah will always forgive.
- The story of Prophet Younus gave us a wonderful example of trusting in Allah.
If we have Allah, we have everything.

Scan QR code! For Revision Notes and Quizzes.

AZHARY PRESS

Rearrange The Story Events!

He was sad and left the city on a ship to find a better place to spread the message.

After Prophet Younus had left, the calm sky over Nineveh turned red.

Allah lifted His punishment, and everyone became a true believer.

He asked Allah to save him, and the whale spat him out at the shore.

Prophet Younus invited the people of Nineveh to worship Allah, but they refused

A storm rocked the boat and Younus (PBUH) was swallowed by a whale.

1. Prophet Younus was born in Gaza, Palestine.

2. Younus (PBUH) left his city without Allah's permission.

3. He was swallowed by a big whale, and he never returned to his city.

4. Prophet Younus was thrown out of the boat to lighten the load.

5. Prophet Younus sought the help of some fishermen who saved him.

6. Most of the people of Nineveh believed in Allah.

7. Allah forgave them and lifted His punishment.

8. Seek forgiveness from Allah; Allah will always forgive.

EXERCISES

Word Search Puzzle!

(Words can be found in any direction, including diagonal, and can overlap each other.)

G	N	I	N	R	A	W	B	E	L	L	Y
P	U	N	I	S	H	M	E	N	T	A	E
O	M	G	U	F	L	Y	D	I	P	U	P
D	O	D	O	O	H	K	P	O	R	G	E
E	H	T	B	R	E	S	C	U	E	H	R
S	E	R	A	G	A	W	H	A	L	E	M
I	R	T	F	A	T	H	E	R	E	D	I
R	I	S	A	U	S	Y	O	U	N	U	S
P	U	N	I	E	S	H	M	A	N	T	S
R	N	O	T	B	A	S	I	L	E	C	I
U	I	U	H	O	W	R	U	P	O	W	O
S	O	R	T	B	H	E	V	E	N	I	N

YOUNUS	NINEVEH	LAUGHED	PERMISSION
SHIP	WHALE	PUNISHMENT	BELLY
RESCUE	SPIT	SKY	RED
FORGAVE	SURPRISED	FAITH	WARNING

EXERCISES

Muhammad (PBUHF)*

We are now in Makkah (Mecca), a mountain village in what is known now as Saudi Arabia. Most people who lived there worshipped idols.

Arabs were known for many good things; they were brave and generous, but they also had problems when it came to equality. Some families were too proud of themselves and belittled others. There was also a lot of fighting.

Prophet Muhammad (PBUHF) was born in Makkah. His father, **Abdullah**, had already died before his birth. His mother, **Lady 'Aminah**, was not well and had to find someone to feed and care for him; **Lady Halimah** did this for two years outside Makkah.

*Peace Be Upon Him and his Family

The two-year-old baby boy then returned to Makkah to be cared for by his mom (Lady 'Aminah) and his maid (**Lady Um Ayman**).

At the age of six, The Prophet's mother died, and his care was moved to his grandfather, **Abdul-Muttalib**. It won't be for long as, after two years only, Abdul-Muttalib died as well.

The eight-year-old boy, then, is cared for by his uncle, **Abu Talib**, who raised and taught him trading and business.

Abu Talib raised and loved The Prophet as one of his children and even more. The Prophet is now a youngster who works as a shepherd and travels with his uncle on business trips to Syria and Yemen.

People in Makkah loved, respected and trusted Muhammad (PBUHF); he was known as "The Honest... The Trustworthy."

Lady Khadijah (RA)*, who is a well-respected, wealthy businesswoman, asked Muhammad (PBUHF) to work for her, and he agreed.

He was such a wonderful man; honest, kind, and trustworthy that she asked to marry him. Muhammad (PBUHF) married her when he was 25, and they had two boys and four girls.

He used to go every year to Hira' Cave on Annour Mountain to think about His Lord who created him and to avoid the idols.

The year he became 40 years old, while he was in the cave thinking, the angel **Jibreel** came down to him with the message of Islam.

The angel commanded Muhammad (PBUHF), "Read". "I can't read", The Prophet replied. The angel repeated the request three times, and Muhammed's reply was the same every time.

*(Radeya-Allahu-'Anha) May Allah be pleased with her.

The first verses of Qur'an were the ones angel Jibreel read to our Prophet (PBUHF):

"Read, ⌜O Prophet,⌝ in the Name of your Lord Who created."

(Al-'Alaq, 1)

Our Prophet (PBUHF) returned home and started delivering Allah's Message to his closest relatives and friends.

After 3 years of telling people secretly about Islam, Allah commanded our Prophet to make The Message public.

The Prophet (PBUHF) climbed Assafa Mountain and told everyone that he was the messenger of Allah, the only true God.

Most people were angry, and his bad uncle, **Abu Lahab**, cursed him. Those who hated Islam started harming the Prophet (PBUHF) and his Muslim followers.

The non-believers started killing the Muslims and planned to kill The Prophet(PBUHF); a man named **'Uqbah** put his sheet around the Prophet's neck and squeezed it very severely while he was praying near The Ka'bah.

اللهم صل على سيدنا محمد

"Abu Bakr came and pulled `Uqbah away from the Prophet and said, "Do you intend to kill a man just because he says: 'My Lord is Allah,."

(Al-Bukhari)

Bilal (RA)*, who refused the idols and accepted Islam, was punished by his master. The evil master threw Bilal on rocks and brought a burning massive rock onto Bilal's body and chest.

The Prophet gave permission to the believers to leave Makkah and move to **Yathrib**.

They had to leave everything behind and start a new life in a different city.

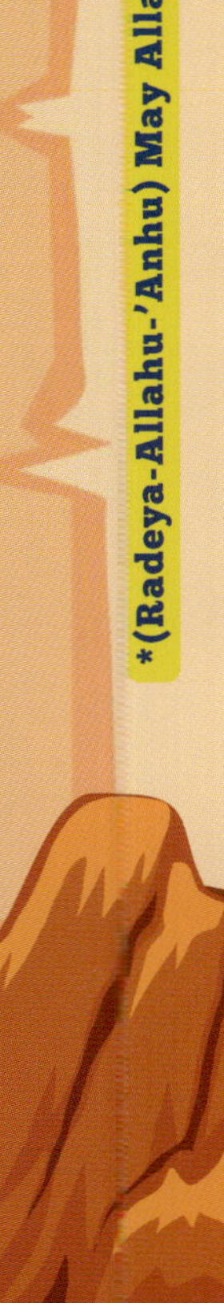

Slowly and secretly the Muslims started to travel to Yathrib.

Abu Bakr (RA) remained behind in Makkah, waiting for the Prophet (PBUHF) to receive the order from Allah Almighty to leave. Abu Bakr prepared two camels for the journey and waited for his dear friend patiently.

JUST IN TIME!

The night Allah permitted our Prophet (PBUHF) to migrate, a group of young men, each one from a tribe of Makkah, stood outside the Prophet's home, waiting to strike him one by one when he comes out and kill him.

Allah the All-Knowing Knew of their plan and guided the Prophet (PBUHF) to safety.

Ali Ibn Abi Talib (RA), the prophet's cousin, stayed in the Prophet's bed till the morning. Muhammad (PBUHF) and Abu Bakr managed to hide in Mount Thawr until Quraysh stopped searching for them.

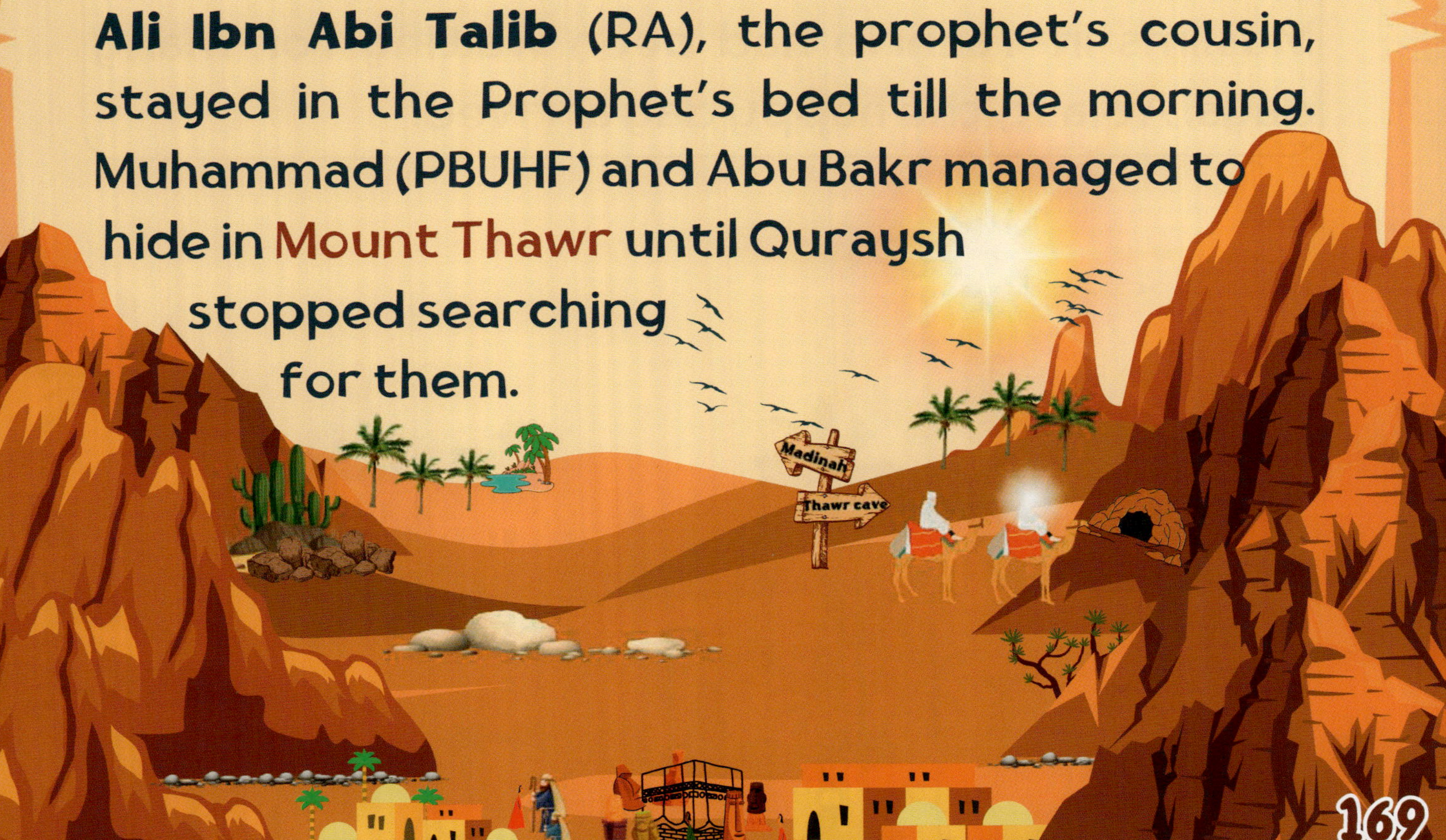

Quraysh offered a big reward to anyone who would bring the Prophet (PBUHF) back, dead or alive. When the Prophet (PBUHF) and Abu Bakr were in the cave, a group of men, trying to get the reward money, came very close to Cave Thawr's entrance during their search. Abu Bakr could see their feet and feared the Prophet (PBUHF) would be found.

The Prophet (PBUHF) comforted him saying: "What do you think of two, whose third is Allah?" The Prophet meant that they should not fear as Allah was with them.

AT LAST!

When the time was right, they left the cave and continued on their long and difficult journey to Madinah.

Muslims in Yathrib had been waiting for many days. At last, the happy day arrived!

When the Prophet (PBUHF) arrived, Muslims followed him as he entered the city, sang songs of joy, and praised Allah.

طلع البدر علينا

Madinah's name was Yathrib but was changed to Al-Madinah Al-Monawarah (The Lit City) because of the light our beloved Prophet (PBUHF) spread all over it.

Muhammad (PBUHF) is the last prophet and messenger.

We must follow our beloved Prophet so Allah can love us.

May Allah's Peace and blessings be upon him and his family.

Scan QR code ! For Revision Notes and Quizzes.

AZHARY PRESS

Rearrange The Story Events!

3 years after receiving Islam, he announced it from the top of Assafa Mountain.

The Prophet and his companions migrated from Makkah to Madinah.

In Madinah, They established a new life and built a mosque.

Some people followed The Prophet and were tortured for becoming Muslims.

Prophet Muhammad was born in Makkah; a city where people worshipped idols.

When he turned 40, Allah revealed to him The Qur'an in Hira' Cave.

EXERCISES

1. Bilal (RA) refused the idols and accepted Islam.

2. Muslims migrated from Jeddah to Madinah.

3. The Prophet's mother is Lady Halimah.

4. The Prophet's grandfather is Abdul-Muttalib.

5. The Prophet was known as the fastest and the strongest.

6. During Hijrah, The Prophet hid in Hira' Cave.

7. Lady Khadijah was a well-respected businesswoman.

8. Abu Lahab supported The Prophet and defended him.

EXERCISES

Word Search Puzzle!

(Words can be found in any direction, including diagonal, and can overlap each other.)

I	Q	B	M	M	O	U	N	T	A	I	N
Y	O	A	Q	A	K	N	A	B	S	L	M
W	A	L	U	D	I	I	Y	D	S	O	A
E	R	Q	R	I	L	T	A	B	A	V	K
B	A	U	A	N	A	M	I	X	F	E	K
E	B	E	Y	A	M	R	A	M	A	U	A
L	I	E	S	A	H	H	A	E	N	R	H
I	A	S	H	T	A	I	M	L	V	W	A
E	Y	U	A	R	R	M	E	A	I	A	G
V	M	Y	J	A	W	A	N	L	R	H	C
E	A	I	M	O	O	N	A	I	F	T	Y
!	H	A	M	I	L	A	H	B	E	H	A

HIRAA	CAVE	ASSAFA	MOUNTAIN
HALIMAH	BILAL	AAMENAH	HIJRAH
MAKKAH	MADINA	YATHRIB	ALI
THAWR	QURAYSH	MUHAMMAD	ARABIA

EXERCISES

7TH

Every journey, no matter how long, eventually reaches its destination. You've arrived at Azhary Exam Island, the final station of your 3rd (First-Class) We Believe Journey aboard the Azhary Press Train.

Here, you'll showcase all the wonderful knowledge you've acquired, organise the landmarks you've visited, and celebrate your exploration.

Revise well and get the highest grades as we eagerly await your participation in our 4th We Believe Journey.

REVISION
AND
RESOURCES

TEACHER

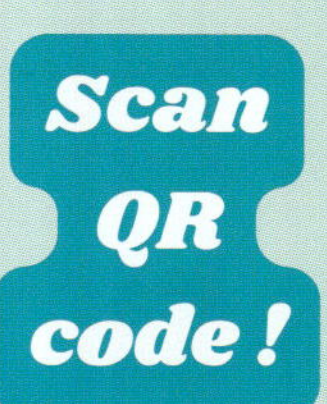
Scan
QR
code !

PARENT

STUDENT

AZHARY EXAMINATION ISLAND

Match the words with the definitions!

- ☐ A part of our wealth that doesn't belong to us
- ☐ 4 Rak'ah Prayer at noon. Qur'an is read silently during it.
- ☐ He is Allah's messenger to His Prophets.
- ☐ 4 Rak'ah Prayer in the night. It is a loud prayer.

1. Scriptures
2. Jibreel
3. Destiny
4. Wudu'
5. Isha'
6. Israfeel
7. Zakah
8. Dhuhr

- ☐ A form of cleanliness we should perform before prayers
- ☐ The sacred books that Allah sent to His messengers
- ☐ Believing that Allah has a special plan for everything
- ☐ He blows the trumpet to signal The Hereafter.

1. Shahadah is the second pillar of Islam.

2. During prayer, we should look at the area of Sujood.

3. We know the exact number of prophets and messengers.

4. Eid-ul-Fitr is right before Ramadan.

5. We start Wudu' by washing our arms.

6. Eid-ul-Adha comes during the month of Dhul-Hijjah.

7. Allah's right upon us is to build a good life.

8. Muslims start prayer by saying Subhan-Allah.

1. Prophet Nouh's ark peacefully landed on Mount Sinai.

2. Your toys are yours only. You shouldn't share with others.

3. When sleeping, lie down on your left or right side.

4. Abu Lahab supported The Prophet and defended him.

5. We call Allah (The Most Merciful) whenever we read Qur'an

6. When we forgive, we give away our rights.

7. Prophet Muhammad (PBUHF) was known as "The Strongest"

8. Prophet Younus sought the help of some fishermen who saved him.

12 Write A Prophet's Name To Match The Story!

Nouh **Younus** **Muhammad**

EXAM 1

Match Arabic with English!

/8

Arabic Treasure

1 Oneness	نَظَافَة
2 Cleanliness	أَخْلَاق
3 Merciful	رَحِيم
4 Hereafter	تَوْحِيد
5 Manners	لِسَان
6 Tongue	رُكْن
7 Miracle	غَيْبَة
8 Pillar	مُعْجِزَة
9 Backbiting	الْآخِرَة

AZHARY EXAMINATION ISLAND

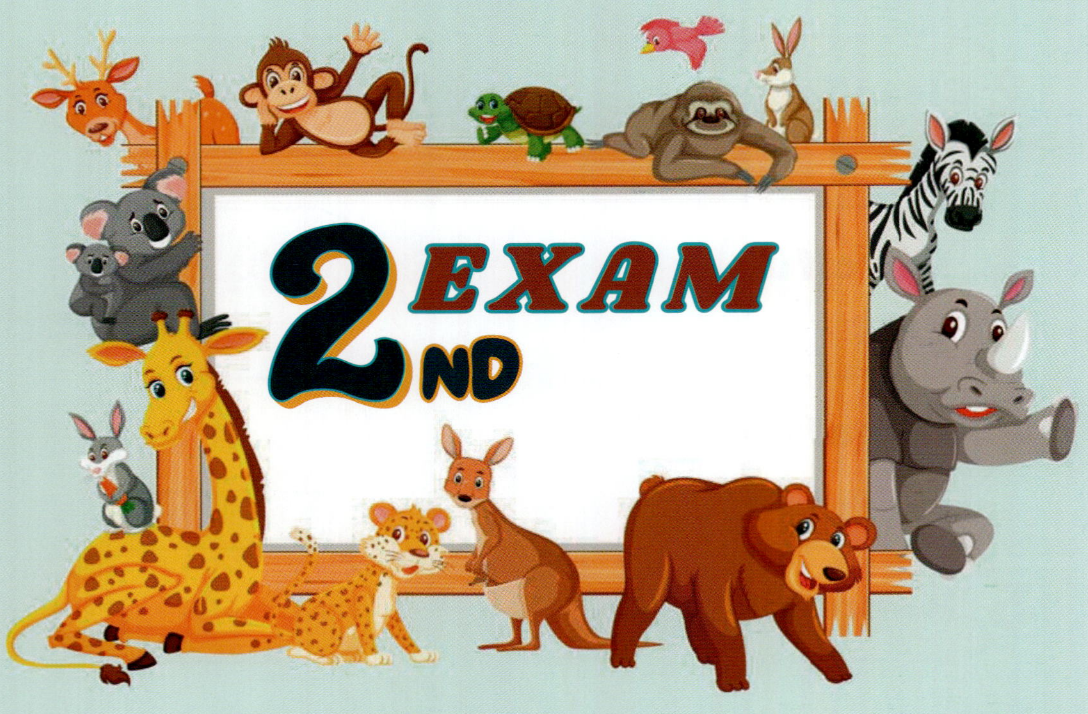

Match the words with the definitions!

/8

3 Rak'ah Prayer after sunset. It is a loud prayer.

1 Hajj

It is a special name for God and is given only to Him

2 Hereafter

Believing that no true god exists except Allah

3 Meekal

The most important pillar of Islam

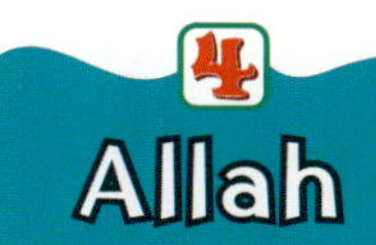

4 Allah

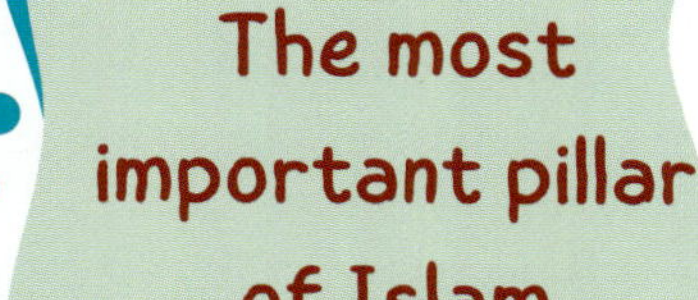

5 Tawheed

The other life which we will be brought back to after we die

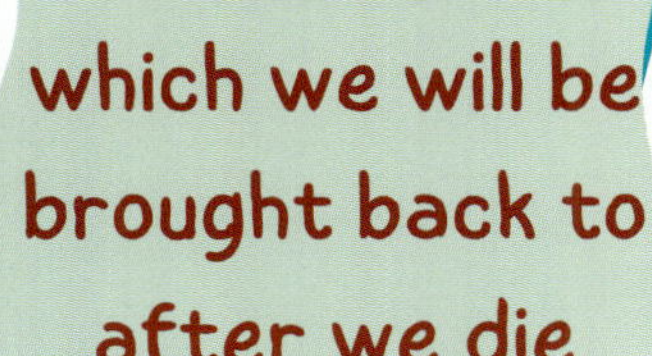

6 Maghrib

The last message Allah sent.It means submission.

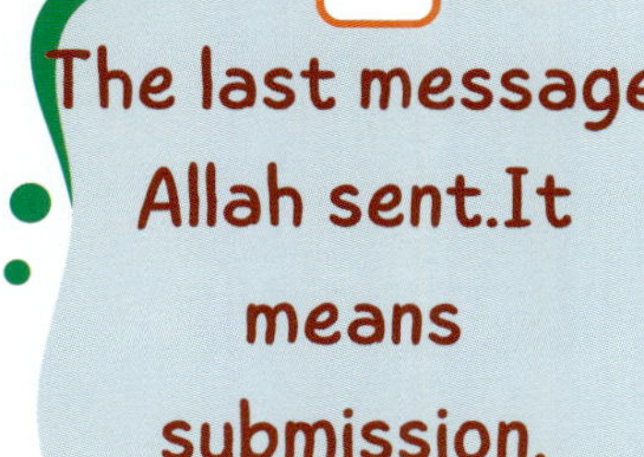

7 Shahadah

A journey to a sacred place

8 Islam

He is the angel of rain and plants.

/8

1. Dressing properly in Islam is a personal preference.

2. The Prophet's mother is Lady Halimah.

3. Allah revealed Surat Al-Mutaffefeen to warn those who lie.

4. You should keep two-thirds of your stomach for food.

5. Prophet Nouh's son listened and survived at the end.

6. Younus (PBUH) left his city without Allah's permission.

7. Al-Ansar gave half their wealth to Al-Mohajereen.

8. Generosity is giving because you have plenty.

1. Lady Khadijah was a well-respected businesswoman.
2. The Bible was sent to Prophet 'Adam.
3. There are seven pillars of Eiman.
4. Prophet Younus was thrown out of the boat to lighten the load.
5. The Muslims of Makkah supported the migrants of Madinah.
6. The first thing we will be asked about in 'Akhirah is Sawm.
7. The pilgrimage must be twice in a lifetime.
8. Allah chose five Prophets to be the most special; Nouh (PBUH) is one of them.

12

Write A Prophet's Name To Match The Story!

Nouh Younus Muhammad

Match Arabic with English!

/8

Arabic Treasure

1 A blessing	أَمَانَة ☐
2 silence	تَعَاوُن ☐
3 Road	تَبَسُّم ☐
4 Lying	طَرِيق ☐
5 Smiling	نِعْمَة ☐
6 Supporters	أَنْصَار ☐
7 Cooperation	صَمْت ☐
8 Trust	كَذِب ☐
9 Evil	شَرّ ☐

WE BELIEVE
COMING SOON
COMPLETE SERIES
AZHARY PRESS
دار أزهري للنشر والتوزيع
Age 3+ Early Years ISLAMIC STUDIES Nursery 1
Age 4+ Early Years ISLAMIC STUDIES Nursery 2
Age 5+ Foundation ISLAMIC STUDIES Guide 1
Age 6+ KS1 ISLAMIC STUDIES GUIDE 2
Age 7+ KS1 ISLAMIC STUDIES GUIDE 3
Age 8+ KS2 ISLAMIC STUDIES GUIDE 4
Age 9+ KS2 ISLAMIC STUDIES GUIDE 5
Age 10+ KS2 ISLAMIC STUDIES GUIDE 6
Age 11+ KS2 ISLAMIC STUDIES GUIDE 7
Age 12+ ISLAMIC STUDIES GUIDE 8
KS3 ISLAMIC STUDIES GUIDE 9
Age 14+ KS3 ISLAMIC STUDIES GUIDE 10
Age 15+ KS4 ISLAMIC STUDIES GUIDE 11
Age 16+ KS4 ISLAMIC STUDIES GUIDE 12
Age 17+ KS5 ISLAMIC STUDIES GUIDE 13
Age 18+ KS5 ISLAMIC STUDIES GUIDE 14
AZHARY PRESS
WE BELIEVE SERIES

AL-HIJRAH TRUST
BIRMINGHAM, UK.

LITTLE MUNCHKIDS
TALHA MESUT

CREATION MOTORS SPORTS
TANWEER HAFEEZ

As we celebrate the launch of the "We Believe" series, a project fueled by passion and purpose, we extend our deepest gratitude to our esteemed partners and sponsors. Your unwavering support has been instrumental in transforming this dream into a reality.

Thanks to your generosity, we can now offer a groundbreaking Islamic education resource to young Muslims worldwide. Your belief in our mission has fueled the creation of a series that ignites intellectual curiosity, strengthens faith, and fosters a love for learning.

We are truly humbled by your commitment to empowering the future generation of our Ummah. Through your partnership, you have played a vital role in ensuring every child has access to engaging and age-appropriate resources that nurture their Islamic understanding.

Words cannot fully express our appreciation for your invaluable contributions. May Allah (SWT) reward you abundantly for your generosity and for placing your trust in our vision.

We look forward to a continued journey of collaboration, shaping the future of Islamic education together.

"AL-HIJRAH TRUST"

We offer a special thanks to the Al-Hijrah Trust, our esteemed partners. Their invaluable financial support and dedication were instrumental in bringing the "We Believe" series to life. The Trust not only provided crucial funding but also served as an essential testing ground for the series. Their Madrasah and dedicated staff played a vital role in refining the curriculum and ensuring its effectiveness for young learners.

With heartfelt thanks,
The "We Believe" Team